Civil Rights in America

Civil Rights in America

A Handbook of Legal History

Daniel McLinden

Universal Publishers
Irvine • Boca Raton

Civil Rights in America:
A Handbook of Legal History

For permission to photocopy or use material electronically from this work,
please access www.copyright.com or contact the Copyright Clearance Center,
Inc. (CCC) at 978-750-8400. CCC is a not-for-profit organization that provides
licenses and registration for a variety of users. For organizations that have been
granted a photocopy license by the CCC, a separate system of payments has been
arranged.

Universal Publishers, Inc.
Irvine • Boca Raton
USA • 2021
www.Universal-Publishers.com

ISBN: 978-1-62734-326-8 (pbk.)
ISBN: 978-1-62734-327-5 (ebk.)

Typeset by Medlar Publishing Solutions Pvt Ltd, India
Cover design by Ivan Popov
Cover illustrations by Daniel McLinden

Library of Congress Cataloging-in-Publication Data

Names: McLinden, Daniel, 1947- author.
Title: Civil rights in America : a handbook of legal history / Daniel
    McLinden.
Description: Irvine : Universal-Publishers, Inc., 2020.
Identifiers: LCCN 2020039771 (print) | LCCN 2020039772 (ebook) |
    ISBN 9781627343268 (paperback) | ISBN 9781627343275 (ebook)
Subjects: LCSH: Civil rights--United States--History.
Classification: LCC KF4749 .M395 2020 (print) | LCC KF4749 (ebook) |
    DDC 342.7308/509--dc23
LC record available at https://lccn.loc.gov/2020039771
LC ebook record available at https://lccn.loc.gov/2020039772

Table of Contents

CHAPTER 1

Overview

General Statement

The needle of America's moral compass has landed on good, evil and everything in between. Slavery made a mockery of the American ideals set out in the *Declaration of Independence* and *US Constitution*.

American courts trampled on civil rights for one hundred fifty years. Then things began to change midway through the 20th century.

"All men are created equal" (*Declaration of Independence* 1776) did not count slaves as men and "Equal protection of the law" (*14th Amendment* 1868) was interpreted by the US Supreme Court to prevent states—but not their White citizens—from discriminating against Blacks.

Civil rights is a struggle. Here is a broad look at it.

Introduction

America is called "the great melting pot"—a land of opportunity—a nation of immigrants—with its prime resource—its people—the most diverse on earth.

Whites came to America for better lives. Blacks came in chains in cargo holds in slave ships.

Whites took land from Native Americans through double-dealing and military offensives.

To complete expansion westward the United States made war on Mexico.

While the Civil War led to deconstruction of the South and an end to slavery, reconstruction did not lead to racial equality.

Civil Rights

Civil rights are defined as the rights of citizens to political and social freedom and equality—the opposite of slavery and human degradation.

The American ideal for civil rights evolved in law from slavery to personal freedom and equal treatment under the law, *i.e.*, freedom from governmental interference in a person's opinions, religious practices, beliefs, and private matters; and, equal treatment of persons regardless of their race, color, ethnicity, national origin, religious beliefs, sex (gender) or sexual orientation.

It took a bloody civil war over slavery to trigger the ideal of equal treatment under the law for Whites and non-Whites embodied in the 14th Amendment (1868).

But court decisions on the 14th Amendment narrowed it to apply to wrongful *state* action only, not *state* inaction or wrongful *private* action. These decisions fostered racial discrimination and led to more segregation laws.

The intended effect of the 14th amendment—racial equality and integration—went dormant for decades until the 1950s when the door opened for court challenges and rulings. Today change continues toward racial equality, gender equality, personal privacy, same sex marriage and sexual orientation.

History

For seventy-six years (1789 to 1865) Whites had rights under the US Constitution (the supreme law of the land) but people of color did not. The Constitution, by ignoring slavery, left the issue of slavery to the States. State sovereignty gave states the power to decide to have slavery or not.

Northern states with small Black populations became free states. Southern states with agrarian economies built on slave labor became slave states.

The territorial footprint of the United States expanded in the 1800s from the Atlantic to the Pacific. White settlers took over Indian and Mexican lands. New states came into the Union. "Manifest Destiny" they called it—America's self-proclaimed divine right to seize all territory from coast to coast.

With expansion, Northerners wanted to add *free* states to the Union; Southerners, *slave* states. The country was deeply divided over the slavery issue.

Missouri Compromise (1820)

The US Constitution (written in 1787 and ratified in 1789) was completely silent as to slavery. It did not use the word "slave" or "slavery" and merely referred to slaves as "other Persons" (*i.e.*, in contrast to "free Persons" or "Indians") in a math formula for apportionment of direct taxes and congressional representation.

There was no discussion of the concept of slavery nor any argument for or against it in the Constitution.

It fell on each (sovereign) State to allow slavery or not. In 1820 Congress passed a law called the Missouri Compromise. The compromise was to allow Missouri to come into the Union as a slave state in exchange for Maine coming in as a free state. All other lands north of Missouri's southern border at 36 degrees 30 minutes latitude—if, and when they became states—would come in as free states.

At that time lands to the north and south of the line were mainly Spanish territory—soon to become part of Mexico when it gained its independence from Spain (1821) the next year.

Within fifteen years (1836) Whites went to Mexican territory (Texas) and fought and formed a republic over its eastern half; Whites went to California and fought and formed a republic there (1846); and, President Polk solidified the United States' western territorial expansion with the Mexican American War (1846–1848) taking from Mexico a vast area of land (in addition to Texas and California) that is now all or part of Oklahoma, Kansas, Colorado, Wyoming, Utah, Nevada, New Mexico, and Arizona.

Despite provisions of the treaty ending the war, Whites did not treat Mexicans in those areas as equals. Over time Mexican Americans were relegated to menial positions and inferior (segregated) schools. (Better education since the 1940s has helped Mexican Americans evolve politically and economically.)

Kansas-Nebraska Act (1854)

In 1854 Congress passed the Kansas-Nebraska Act overturning the Missouri Compromise to the extent Kansas and Nebraska—located on land designated "free" by the Missouri Compromise—would not come in as free states pursuant to the Missouri Compromise—but would hold elections on the question whether they would declare themselves free or slave states—so-called popular sovereignty.

Dred Scott Decision (1857)

In 1857 the United States Supreme Court decided the *Dred Scott* case. The Court held Dred Scott, a slave, did not have standing to sue for his freedom because the US Constitution gave him no rights. He was not a *person* under the Constitution rather *property* (of a White person). According to the Court, Scott's presence or residence in a free state or territory was not enough to establish his freedom.

In that year (1857) the people of the United States were at odds over the question of slavery and the outcome of the *Dred Scott* case. Abolitionists deplored the Court decision. And it, along with the national debate over the extension of slavery into new territories, laid the groundwork for civil war.

Civil War (1861–1865)

The political divide over slavery led to a new political party (Republican) against slavery expansion. Its candidate for President, Abraham Lincoln, won the vote in 1860. He did not stress ending slavery but only ending its expansion into new territories. After he was elected, southern states withdrew (seceded) from the Union.

This triggered the Civil War (1861 to 1865) between the northern states that stayed in the Union and fought to preserve it, and the southern states that left it to form their own alliance called the Confederate States of America.

The death toll in the Civil War was 655,000.

In 1865 the Confederacy lost the Civil War and surrendered to the Union, Lincoln was assassinated only days later, and the 13th Amendment was ratified ending slavery.

Southern revisionists have attempted to rewrite history by falsely claiming the war was fought for states' rights—when in fact it was clearly over slavery.

Civil War Amendments to the Constitution aka Reconstruction Amendments

Three amendments came out of the Civil War. They were designed to protect individuals from governmental interference and to recognize basic human rights—the 13th, 14th and 15th Amendments.

The 13th *abolished slavery and involuntary servitude.*

The 14th *applied 5th Amendment due process requirements to states and gave equal protection under the law.* Every person, White or non-White, was to get equal treatment under the law. Despite this constitutional mandate the amendment's aims were subverted by the courts for nearly a century and some states' efforts to disadvantage people of color and other groups continue today.

The 15th *gave freed Black men the right to vote.* (It would take another 50 years (1920) and the 19th Amendment for women to get it.)

Reconstruction (1865–1877)

In 1863 Lincoln signed the Emancipation Proclamation freeing slaves and he initiated a plan in very small measure to export freed slaves to Africa and Central America. He also invited Black soldiers into the Union Army.

Frederick Douglass, a runaway and emancipated slave, was the most well-known Black of his day—writer, orator, journalist, religious abolitionist and forward thinker (also standing for women's rights). He counseled Lincoln, participated in the Underground Railroad, worked for Black recruitment in the Union Army, rebuffed Lincoln's "back to Africa" idea, but believed Lincoln was deep down a true abolitionist.

Lincoln did not live for the Reconstruction era (1865 to 1877). The Reconstruction Act passed over presidential veto (Andrew Johnson) in 1867. It was a time to rebuild the South—thoroughly devastated by war after the Union Army's scorched earth policy—and put Blacks on par with Whites.

Blacks voted and gained political and economic power. But long denied educations, few could read or write. Efforts to school Blacks got underway. Northerners poured into the South, some to help with schooling but most to profit from reconstruction. Southerners derided their opportunism—calling them *carpetbaggers* (since the luggage they came with was made of carpeting material)—and they called their Southern collaborators, *scalawags* (a term first meaning a farm animal of little value then a worthless person).

At every turn the South resisted putting Blacks on equal footing with Whites.

Paramilitary groups, mainly southern Civil War veterans, set fires to Black neighborhoods, kidnapped, lynched and murdered Blacks, and intimidated Black voters, Black politicians and White sympathizers. The Ku Klux Klan (KKK) was formed in Tennessee, the Redshirts in Mississippi and the White League in Louisiana.

Congress passed legislation in 1870 known as the Ku Klux Klan Act to protect freedmen's right to vote, hold office, serve on juries, and get equal protection under the law. The act was strengthened in 1871 to empower the President (Grant) to declare martial law, impose heavy penalties against terrorist organizations and use military force to put down the KKK and other white supremacists.

Grant mainly succeeded but the Redshirts of Mississippi extended their influence to South Carolina and North Carolina. And on voting days Redshirts on horseback brandished weapons and threatened and intimidated Blacks and other Republican voters.

Reconstruction failed.

The Ku Klux Klan drifted into the shadows but reemerged throughout the South and other pockets of the country after the 1915 film "The Birth of a Nation" vilifying Blacks and glorifying the Confederacy and the Klan. The Klan came out again against Blacks. Klan members hid behind their white hoods and robes.

Bound by racism and bigotry they operated in the dead of night and got away with burning crosses on Black front yards, beating, lynching and murdering Blacks.

What initially looked like racial gains were replaced with pervasive segregation, and suppression of black education, voting and economic opportunity. Legislative and judicial oppression, harsh treatment, illiteracy and poverty remained at the core of Black life.

And not just in the South.

Other Setbacks to Freedom

After the Civil War, its amendments, and the Civil Rights Acts of 1866, 1870, 1871 and 1875, the emerging goal was to treat all persons equally under the law. But courts, including the US Supreme Court, found ways to gut the notion of social equality.

The Court interpreted "equal protection" of Whites and Blacks under the 14th Amendment to prohibit *state* discrimination but not *private* (individuals) discrimination.

The Court's refusal to apply the 14th Amendment to *all* discriminatory action both *state* and *private* led states—mainly but not entirely in the South—to enact more discriminatory laws (the Black Codes and Jim Crow laws—derogatorily named after a theatrical character depicting a slave and a traditional slave song "Jump Jim Crow").

These laws aimed at Blacks restricted education, the right to travel, vote, testify in court, and sit on juries, among other things, giving greater impetus to an era rife with the badges, incidents and vestiges of slavery. These laws promoted segregation based on skin color.

It was not until the mid-20th century when courts began to stand up for equal protection.

The struggle did not end there. Southern and conservative states continued to enact laws undermining individual freedoms by, among other things, suppressing voting rights, limiting reproductive rights, and denying individuals' basic rights because of their sexual orientation.

Slavery (1619–1865)

Slavery existed in America from when slaves were first brought to Jamestown, Virginia (1619) and continued through America's declaration of independence (1776), writing (1787) and ratification of the US Constitution (1789), and the Civil War (ending in 1865).

Slaves, denied basic human rights, were prisoners of their White masters. Slavery was marked by mental, physical and sexual abuse. Slaves were roundly denied education, the right to marry, or control of their children. They lived and died in extreme poverty under the White man's whip with no civil rights. A very small minority were freed or escaped to the North.

Slavery lasted 246 years in North America.

Juneteenth (short for "June Nineteenth") marks the day when federal troops arrived in Galveston, Texas in 1865 to take control of the state and make sure Blacks were set free. The troops' arrival came two and a half years after the signing of the Emancipation Proclamation (January 1, 1863). Juneteenth honors the end to slavery in the US and is considered the longest-running African American holiday.

Indigenous People (Native Americans–American Indians)

Native Americans populated the New World before the White man came. Their population was drastically reduced through contact with the White man.

Two things caused the American Indian population to go from an estimated 12 to 15 million with the arrival of Columbus (1492) to 237,000 by 1900:

(1) American Indians lacked immunities to European diseases; this accounted for the majority of their deaths—primarily from smallpox but from other diseases including measles, influenza, whooping cough, diphtheria, typhus, bubonic plague, cholera, and scarlet fever; and,

(2) westward continental expansion and the influx of European immigrants in the 1800s led the US to turn Indian land into new territories and states, force relocation of Indian nations and tribes, and war with and massacre the ones who fought to stand their ground.

Indian braves who fought back were often ferocious in their killing and mutilation of Whites.

Formal US policy was *not* to annihilate the Indian (genocide) but fraudulently induced and broken treaties creating and shrinking reservation land, together with the US Army's politically sanctioned efforts at warring with the Indian, appeared aimed at just that.

Asian Americans

Asians in the United States have been the object of racial prejudice, unjust laws and court rulings. Asians first began to emigrate to the US in the mid-19th century to work in the West in gold fields and on railroads under dangerous conditions made worse by severe cold and heat.

Like slaves and other immigrant groups they did the pick-and-shovel-hard-labor jobs that built America. Fifteen to twenty thousand Chinese worked on the first transcontinental railroad.

Hundreds of their lives were lost in blasting accidents laying track and tunneling through the solid rock of western mountains.

Since coming to America, Asians have undergone violent and unjust discrimination but now have mainly overcome it.

Asians' unjust treatment included laws barring them from testifying in court and preventing them from becoming citizens; their immigration to America was cut off for years and otherwise restricted; Whites burned down China towns, rioted against Chinese, excluded Asians from union jobs; and, the US government conducted a race-based wartime internment (imprisonment) of Japanese Americans including those who were US citizens at the time.

With respect to Covid 19 in 2020 persons of Asian descent were verbally abused, name-called, coughed and spat on, even physically assaulted, as the coronavirus continued to upend American life. As political rhetoric blaming China for the coronavirus escalated from the US President (Trump) and others, law enforcement officials and human rights advocates saw increasing numbers of hate crimes and incidents of harassment against Asians.

This came at a time when Asians were the biggest immigration group in the United States just ahead of Hispanics (mainly from Mexico and Central America).

Civil Rights and the Courts

The history of civil rights in America is reflected in its laws and court decisions calculated to engender fairness and overcome racial and other kinds of widespread injustice.

But laws and court decisions do not always translate into practice.

The United States Supreme Court has the power to interpret the Constitution. The interpretation of the Constitution usually occurs on a case by case basis.

Unless a provision in the Constitution gets tested in court its legal significance is unsettled. Likewise, a federal law or state law enacted by Congress or a state legislature may or may not be in conflict with the Constitution. Whether or not the law is in conflict can only be determined after it has been challenged in court.

Regarding civil rights, there has been discrimination against persons based on race, color, national origin, religion, sex (gender), sexual orientation, age, and disabilities. The Supreme Court has had opportunities to end such discrimination.

Often, early on, the Court failed to do so. Yet over time both legislation and court decisions have increasingly done so.

Assignment

Write a summary of Chapter 1 in your own words. Also, for upcoming assignments, if you have not briefed a case it would be helpful to familiarize yourself with a briefing method. As students of history and students of law it is essential to know how to brief a case.

Traditionally the method for briefing a case is referred to by the acronym IRAC. IRAC stands for Issue Rule Argument Conclusion.

Issue—The key legal question(s) in the case phrased in the form of a question.

Rule—The source(s) of law relevant to the issue.

Argument—A discussion blending the law and facts of the case in a logical progression toward a legal or equitable conclusion.

Conclusion—The decision reached in the case.

Some briefers use FIRAC. It starts with the facts of the case and proceeds with IRAC.

Here is an example of FIRAC using *Garner v. Louisiana (1961)* a sit-in civil rights case:

Facts: John Burrell Garner, a Black student and two Black friends sat at the White lunch counter of Sitman's Drug Store in

Baton Rouge, Louisiana. The store owner having lunch at the same counter asked them to move to the Black counter across the store but they refused. They just sat there. They were still just sitting there when police officers arrived after the store owner finished his lunch and called them. The police arrested Garner and the others for disturbing the peace.

Issue: Did Garner violate the Louisiana "disturbing the peace" statute?

Rules: Louisiana "disturbing the peace" statute and 14th Amendment

Argument: The Louisiana statute lists several examples of disturbing the peace (fighting, drunk in public, violent conduct by three or more persons, unlawful assembly, interrupting a lawful assembly, or committing any other act to unreasonably disturb or alarm the public).

Garner did none of these things. There is no evidence in the record of any conduct except sitting at Sitman's. Absent evidence against a person no person can be lawfully convicted.

Due process requires any conviction be based on substantial evidence. The 14th Amendment applies due process requirements to the states.

Here the conviction without evidence under the state "disturbing the peace" statute amounted to a denial of due process.

Conclusion: The Lousiana court judgment is reversed.

CHAPTER 2

Courts, Slavery
and Discrimination

Dred Scott v. Sandford (1857)

Dred Scott, a slave, sued for freedom on the ground that he had temporarily resided in a free state (Illinois) and free territory (Wisconsin). The Court found the Missouri Compromise (1820), and a prior Congressional act (1787) establishing free territories around the Great Lakes, unconstitutional because the Constitution itself did not give Congress power to regulate slavery in any state or territory (as the Missouri Compromise and the 1787 congressional act purported to do).

The Court also found the Constitution did not consider persons of African descent citizens entitled to any rights or protections under it. The Court found slaves personal "property" of their owners.

The Court denied Scott his freedom.

[Context—Most slaves never got to travel. At that time establishing a presence or residency in some free states was a means to a slave's freedom under that state's law. The Chief Justice's refusal to recognize a Black as a person underscored his lack of humanity and moral failure to dignify individuals of color. It was a ruling for slaveholders, slavery expansionists, and those Americans who degraded and exploited Blacks for economic and other reasons.]

United States v. Cruikshank (1876)

This case involved the disputed 1872 Louisiana gubernatorial election and the Colfax massacre. The outcome of the election was still in doubt when months later on Easter Sunday 1873 hundreds of freedmen (Black Republicans), some armed and part of the state militia, assembled around the Grant Parish Courthouse in Colfax to protect it from a much more heavily-armed white militia hell-bent on taking it over.

By next day the white militia had lost three members but had killed between an estimated 60 to 150 freedmen. It was a hateful crazed slaughter made more deranged by the murder of Blacks after surrender and after being taken prisoners.

Cruikshank and others were charged with murder, violation of the Klan Act (Enforcement Act of 1870) (*i.e.*, conspiring to deprive freedmen of federal constitutional rights), depriving them of their freedom to assemble (1st Amendment), their right to bear arms (2nd Amendment), and depriving them of their lives under the 14th Amendment.

The majority opinion of the US Supreme Court based its decision on its interpretation of the country's political system with its built-in duality marked by state and federal sovereignty.

The Court found freedom of assembly and the right to bear arms to predate the Constitution. The Court rationalized that these constitutionally protected rights found in the Bill of Rights protected an aggrieved party not from private citizens acting to deny them such rights but only from Congress if it were to act in some way to deny these rights.

The Court also found that 14th Amendment protection meant the federal government guaranteed a persons' rights would not be infringed by state action—a guaranty that did not extend to private (individual) action—and here there was no state action only private action.

The Court found the Klan Act claims misguided or not sufficiently framed.

The court rejected the claims and reversed the convictions.

[Context: The case went from local courthouse massacre to US Supreme Court massacre.

It was a ruling for the Klan.

It emboldened white paramilitary groups to terrorize Blacks. Federal efforts to protect Black civil rights had evaporated.

Reconstruction was over.

The Supreme Court took the language "No state ... shall ... deprive any person of life, liberty, or property [or] deny to any person within its jurisdiction equal protection of the laws" in the 14th Amendment literally, applying it to *state* action only (No *state* shall) and not to (the murderers') *private* actions.

Later decisions relented somewhat in allowing the 1st and 2nd Amendments to apply to state action instead of congressional action only.

But overall the 14th Amendment stood for equal protection for *all* but only as to *state* wrongdoing and not *private* wrongdoing.

The question in the first instance is "Does 'No state shall deprive [or] deny' refer specifically and narrowly to the action of a state or does it mean that no state shall allow deprivation or denial of rights to any person within its jurisdiction BY ANYONE—NOT JUST THE STATE?"

By narrowing the interpretation to state action only, the Supreme Court sanctioned discrimination BY ANYONE except the State—effectively saying NO to racial parity and shoving "equal rights" out the door. It was not OK for a State to discriminate against someone based on color but it was still OK for anyone else to discriminate based on color.

By leaving it to the states to charge and try private bad actors with racial crimes the US Supreme Court was choking the life out of justice in those states with all-white judges and juries still reeling from the outcome of the Civil War.]

Assignment

Draft short biographies of Dred Scott and Roger B. Taney.

CHAPTER 3

Nearly Twenty Years After the Civil War and No Equality for Blacks

The Civil Rights Cases (1883)

The Civil Rights Act (CRA) of 1875 affirmed the equality of all persons in the enjoyment of transportation facilities, hotels, inns, theaters and places of public amusement.

In five consolidated cases, each plaintiff (a Black) unsuccessfully argued that such places though privately owned were essentially public in nature and thus should have been subject to the CRA and 14th Amendment.

As in *United States v. Cruikshank (1876)* the Court differentiated between state and private action, with the majority finding the 14th Amendment to prohibit discriminatory action by a state but not by a private person.

The lone dissenter, Justice John Marshall Harlan, was for a broader interpretation of the 13th and 14th Amendments. He pointed to the public function that privately-owned places of accommodation serve and argued that the line between state and private action is often blurred, for example, how private railroads provide the government function of facilitating travel.

[Context: The 14th Amendment solidified new rights for ex-slaves presumably to enjoy life shoulder to shoulder with Whites. But the Supreme Court drew a line between *state action* and *private action* essentially concluding equal protection under the law meant people of all races should be treated the same by the state only but private (rather than state) discrimination was OK. In effect, this approach continued to foster the inequality of the races.]

United States v. Harris (1883)

Four black men were taken out of a Crockett County, Tennessee jail by a group led by Sheriff R. G. Harris and 19 others (all KKK members). The four men were beaten and one was killed. A deputy sheriff tried to stop the group but failed.

The rule of law in issue in the case was Section 2 of the Force Act of 1871 (aka the Klan Act). The Court found the law unconstitutional on the theory that an Act to enforce the Equal Protection Clause applied only to state action, not to state inaction (failure to protect prisoners).

The Court also held that it was unconstitutional for the federal government to penalize crimes such as assault and murder. It declared that only the local governments have the power to penalize these crimes.

[Context: The Court found for the Klan and the sheriff acting with them. The Court turned several legal and moral principles on their heads.

This court, like the *Cruikshank* court continued to interpret the 14th Amendment the same way, washing its hands of violence against freedmen, and leaving states free to turn blind eyes to injustices against them.]

Assignment

Summarize the successes and failures of Reconstruction.

CHAPTER 4

Inequality–"Separate but Equal"–Segregation–Exclusion v. Equality–Integration–Inclusion

Plessy v. Ferguson (1896)

Louisiana enacted the Separate Car Act in 1890 requiring railroads to run separate railway cars to segregate Black passengers from White.

In 1892 Homer Plessy, who was seven-eighths White, agreed to participate in a test to challenge the Act. He was recruited by the *Comite des Citoyens* (Committee of Citizens), a group of New Orleans residents who sought to repeal the Act.

The group asked Plessy, who was technically Black under Louisiana law (a person with any Black blood), to sit in a "Whites Only" section of a Louisiana train car.

The railroad cooperated with the group in the staging of Plessy's arrest because it thought the Act imposed unnecessary costs on it for the added railway cars.

When Plessy was told to vacate the Whites-Only section he refused and was arrested.

In a 7-1 decision, the Supreme Court ruled against Plessy rejecting his 13th and 14th Amendment arguments even though the legislative Act in question, like any state-made law, constituted state action.

The Court, instead, put its stamp of approval on the doctrine of "separate but equal." This doctrine promoted segregation so long as the separate facility (*e.g.*, the train car here or hypothetically a school) for the Black was substantially equal in quality to that of the White.

According to the majority if a state provided separate but equal facilities for Blacks and Whites it satisfied the requirement of equal protection of the laws under the 14th Amendment.

The dissent, written by Justice John Marshall Harlan, argued that segregationist laws indoctrinate society with the belief that the two races are not equal. He argued that segregationist legislation, like the Louisiana law in this case, assumes "colored citizens are so inferior and degraded that they cannot be allowed to sit in public coaches occupied by white citizens."

These laws promoted and perpetuated the belief that African Americans were inferior to whites, according to Justice Harlan. They must be struck down, he argued, because the government could not "permit the seeds of race hate to be planted under the sanction of law."

Justice Harlan believed that the constitution must be "color-blind," and that it could allow "no superior, dominant ruling class of citizens." Because segregation had the effect of creating such classes, he judged, it was unconstitutional.

[Context: Here the Louisiana law (like any state law) was state action. Equal rights (guaranteed by the 14th Amendment) means Whites and Blacks have equal access to all of the benefits provided by a state (including public transportation and education). Segregating races in America implied unequal treatment of them under the law. The impact of the decision was tremendous and widespread leading to the proliferation of Jim Crow laws designed to hold down Blacks and strangle their economic and educational opportunities.]

Murray v. Pearson (1936)

Donald Gaines Murray sought admission to the University of Maryland School of Law, but his application was rejected on account of his race. The rejection letter stated, "The University of Maryland does not admit Negro students and your application is accordingly rejected."

The letter also acknowledged the university's duty under the *Plessy v. Ferguson (1896)* doctrine of "separate but equal" to assist him in studying in a Black law school (but Maryland did not have one) so it offered to pay for his tuition at a law school located out-of-state. Murray appealed this rejection to the Board of Regents of the university but was refused admittance.

Murray's case was initiated by the Alpha Phi Alpha Fraternity (a Black fraternity) as a fundamental part of its broadening social program. To bolster the fraternity's efforts, it hired Belford Lawson—a famous lawyer. However, by the time the case reached court, Murray was represented by Thurgood Marshall and Charles Hamilton Houston of the Baltimore National Association for the Advancement of Colored People (NAACP). Thurgood Marshall had also been denied admission to the school years before.

Thurgood Marshall argued that the policy of segregation based on race was unconstitutional. He went on to argue that in principle because the state of Maryland had no law school for African Americans much less one separate but equal to its White school Murray had to be admitted.

The judge issued a writ of mandamus, ordering that Pearson, president of the University, admit Murray. The ruling was appealed to the Maryland Court of Appeals, which affirmed the lower court's ruling in January 1936.

The court ruled unanimously not to outlaw segregation in education, but to force the state to honor the 14th Amendment to the US Constitution (as interpreted through the separate but equal doctrine of *Plessy*) to provide substantially equal treatment in the facilities it offers from public funding.

But because the state of Maryland chose only to offer one law school for use by students in the state, that law school was required to be made available to all students regardless of race.

The decision was never taken to the United States Supreme Court. As such, the ruling was not ruled binding outside of the state.

The NAACP's strategy of attacking segregation by demanding equal access to public educational facilities that were not duplicated for Blacks was followed in later legal cases.

[Context: The dismal educational facilities and opportunities for Blacks and their bleak economic conditions produced few students with sufficient academic credentials or ability to pay for higher education.

The NAACP was founded to fight discrimination based on color. Charles Hamilton Houston, heading up the NAACP, was Black, a Northerner, a WWI veteran, a lawyer and law professor, who came up with the strategy to attack the pocketbooks of states that had not built separate and equal schools of higher education for Blacks.

To mount the attack the NAACP took grassroots donations from Blacks and others, mostly in small amounts, from all over the country. Houston saw Murray as a very promising plaintiff. Houston hired a former law student of his from Howard University (a Black school), Thurgood Marshall, and went forward with an attack on discrimination (and segregation) aimed at state's treasuries.]

Assignment

Write a brief history of the NAACP.

CHAPTER 5

Targeting Blacks and Asians

Smith v. Allwright (1944)

The Texas Democratic Party had a rule in place allowing *only* white people to vote in Democratic primaries. Lonnie Smith, a black Texas voter, sued election officials in his county for denying him the right to vote in the Democratic primary in 1940, under the 14th and 15th Amendments of the US Constitution.

The county election officials argued that Smith did not have a constitutional right to vote in the Democratic primary because the Democratic primary was run by a volunteer party organization, not the State of Texas. And because the Democratic party was not a governmental organization it fell outside the reach of the Constitution which is to protect interference from governmental (state) action only—not private action.

The District Court denied Smith's case. The Fifth Circuit Court of Appeal affirmed the District Court's decision, finding that it must follow the US Supreme Court case in *Grovey v. Townsend*, which held that a political party is not an arm of, or agent of, the State for constitutional purposes to establish state action.

The US Supreme Court granted the petition for writ of certiorari (*i.e.*, agreed to hear the case). The Supreme Court overturned *Grovey* and held it was a violation of the 14th and 15th Amendments to deny a person the right to vote in a primary based on race, and a political party running a primary election acts as an agent of the State for constitutional purposes (satisfying the state-action requirement).

The 14th and 15th Amendments are clear that no citizen should be denied the right to vote because of race. County officials in this case argued the Democratic party was a voluntary, non-governmental organization, but the Court found the party acted for the state.

With the State permitting the Democratic party to allow only white voters to participate in the Democratic primary the State is acting in violation of the Constitution by denying to Blacks equal protection under the law.

[Context: Southern states as a voting block had been solidly Democrat for decades since the Civil War. Whoever won a Democratic primary would go on to win a general election.

Keeping Black voters from voting in primaries meant they would have no say in who the proposed candidate should be. What if the congressional district were 90% Black? That district would likely vote for a Black in a primary and again in a general election.

But Blacks were blocked from voting their interests in the first instance (the primary election). This meant the state would keep pumping out White candidates only.

The Supreme Court that had always required state action (rather than private action) to enforce 14th Amendment equal protection hung its hat on a solid "agency" principle imputing the political party's conduct to the state.

This was a crack in the wall of racial inequality.]

Korematsu v. United States (1944)

On December 7, 1941 the Japanese made a surprise aerial attack on the US Navy fleet docked in Pearl Harbor, Hawaii. The next day the US declared war on Japan—and a few days later—on the other Axis Powers (Germany and Italy).

Within months President Franklin D. Roosevelt signed Executive Order 9066 granting the secretary of war and his commanders the power "to prescribe military areas in such places and of such extent as he or the appropriate Military Commander may determine, from which any or all persons may be excluded."

This laid the groundwork for Civilian Exclusion Order No. 34 by the Commanding General of the Western Defense Command, directing the exclusion after May 9, 1942, from a described West Coast military area (the West Coast) all persons of Japanese ancestry to protect against their potential espionage and sabotage.

Individuals and whole families (parents, grandparents and children) were imprisoned in internment camps—taking with them only what they could carry and leaving behind all other possessions and the land they owned.

Fred Korematsu, 23, of Japanese descent, had been born in Oakland, California. He defied the order and was arrested. His case went to the US Supreme Court. On December 18, 1944, in a 6-3 decision the US Supreme Court upheld the conviction.

Writing for the majority, Justice Hugo L. Black argued: Compulsory exclusion of large groups of citizens from their homes, except under circumstances of direst emergency and peril, is inconsistent with our basic governmental institutions. But when, under conditions of modern warfare, our shores are threatened by hostile forces, the power to protect must be commensurate with the threatened danger.

Dissenting from the majority were Justices Owen Roberts, Frank Murphy and Robert H. Jackson. Jackson's dissent is particularly critical: "Korematsu was born on our soil, of parents born in Japan. The Constitution makes him a citizen of the United States by nativity, and a citizen of California by residence. No claim is made that he is not loyal to this country. There is no suggestion that, apart from the matter involved here, he is not law-abiding and well disposed. Korematsu, however, has been convicted of an act not commonly a crime. It consists merely of being present in the state whereof he is a citizen, near the place where he was born, and where all his life he has lived."

On the same day as the Korematsu decision, in *Ex parte Endo* the Court sidestepped the constitutionality of internment as a policy but forbade the government to detain a US citizen whose loyalty was recognized by the US government.

Post script: In 2011 the solicitor general of the United States confirmed that one of his predecessors, who had argued for the government in *Korematsu* and in an earlier related case, *Hirabayashi* v. *United States* (1943), had deceived the Court by suppressing a report by the Office of Naval Intelligence that concluded that Japanese Americans did not pose a threat to US national security.

And in *Trump* v. *Hawaii* (2018) the US Supreme Court explicitly repudiated and effectively overturned the *Korematsu* decision, characterizing it as "gravely wrong the day it was decided" and "overruled in the court of history."

Moreover, no Japanese American was ever convicted of espionage or sabotage. And the most decorated US Army unit for its size in World War II was the 442nd Regiment made up of Japanese Americans fighting in Europe.

[Context: The sneak attack on Pearl Harbor outraged America.

But forced imprisonment of Japanese American citizens and their families was an unconstitutional race-based response. Allowing the internees to bring only what they could carry and jeopardizing their wealth was also unconstitutional.

Sequestering them during war time turned out unnecessary to protect the war effort—but it likely protected them from the harm and atrocities they might have suffered in their own homes from an historically racist public.

In 1999, efforts of the Japanese American Citizens League bore some fruit when the government paid reparations to internees (82,219 Japanese Americans) and their heirs ($20,000 each) for the internment found to have been the product of racism.]

Assignment

Describe what life was like for Japanese Americans in America before, during and after internment at Manzanar (1942–1945).

CHAPTER 6

Unequal Schools and Restrictive Covenants

Mendez v. Westminster (1947)

After *Plessy v. Ferguson (1896)* it was common practice to have separate schools for African Americans or Mexican Americans and Anglos (Whites). The *Mendez v. Westminster School District* case (1947) was pivotal in ending segregation of Mexican American school children in California.

At the turn of the 20th century, Mexican American children in the Southwest were separated from Anglo school children and segregated into "Mexican" schools.

The Mexican schools were often outbuildings or barns rather than institutional structures equal to those of "Anglo" schools. The Mexican schools did not get as many supplies or the newer books Anglo schools got.

In 1945 the Mendezes tried to enroll their children into the Main Street Elementary School located in the Westminster School

District, Orange County, California. Main Street School was an Anglo school. The children were turned away from the school and sent to Hoover School, a "Mexican" elementary school.

Led by the Mendezes, other parents of Mexican American children joined them to file a class action lawsuit in the Los Angeles federal court on behalf of 5,000 families for segregating their children.

The case became known as the *Mendez v. Westminster School District.* The Mendez's counsel, David Marcus, a Los Angeles attorney was sought after and funded by the League of United Latin American Citizens (LULAC).

Marcus argued in court for desegregation of California's schools "on the grounds that perpetuation of school admissions on the basis of race or nationality violated the Fifth and Fourteenth Amendments of the National Constitution."

In response, the defendant school districts argued that Mexican children were unfit and incapable to attend the "Anglo" school.

The defense claimed that the Mexican American children possessed contagious diseases, had poor moral habits, were inferior in their personal hygiene, spoke only Spanish and lacked English speaking skills making them unqualified to attend Anglo schools and facilities.

Despite heavy opposition from the Anglo Orange County community and school districts, in 1946, federal judge Paul J. McCormick ruled in favor of the Mendezes and the co-plaintiffs.

McCormick found that "the segregation of Mexican Americans in public schools was a violation of the state law" and unconstitutional under the Fourteenth Amendment because of the denial of due process and equal protection. The judge struck down systematic segregation in public schools in California.

Shortly after Judge McCormick's ruling, in April 1947 the defense sought to appeal the decision claiming the federal court did not have the authority in this matter. Plaintiffs' representation mushroomed on the appeal level.

With financial support from LULAC and continued legal representation from Marcus, newly added support came from several multiracial organizations, such as, the National Association for the Advancement of Colored People, American Jewish Congress, American Civil Liberties Union, and the Japanese American Citizens League. (Not surprisingly, NAACP Attorney Thurgood Marshall used his experience in *Mendez* to soon after pursue desegregation for African Americans in *Brown v. Board of Education (1954)*.)

The Court of Appeals supported Judge McCormick's earlier decision: segregation of Mexican American children violated the Fourteenth Amendment.

McCormick's decision ushered in the end of segregation and a new bill, entitled "The Anderson Bill" that passed the California Assembly and the Senate and was signed into law by California Governor Earl Warren in June 1947. By September that same year Mexican American children were now able to attend integrated schools throughout the state.

The *Mendez v. Westminster School District* case broke down legalized segregation and shined a light on conditions of systematic racism and discrimination, prevalent not only in California but the rest of the country.

[Context: The war was over. Mexican Americans had served and sacrificed for their country. They were taxpayers. They were entitled to what their tax dollars provided. Like all parents Mexican Americans wanted the best for their children.

The formula that worked for the Mendezes required a minority population tired of being treated second-class, brave parents and children, a compassionate lawyer (charitably funded by Mexican American donors), and a judge with basic humanity. Sometimes, like this time, justice prevails.]

Shelley v. Kraemer (1948)

Kraemer and other white property owners governed by a restrictive covenant (precluding the sale of properties to Blacks or Asians) brought suit in Missouri state court seeking to block the Shelley family, who were African American, from owning property burdened by the restriction.

The Kraemers lost at trial, but on appeal the Missouri Supreme Court reversed and ruled that the restrictive covenant was effective and that it did not violate the Shelleys' constitutional rights. The Shelleys then appealed the case to the United States Supreme Court.

The US Supreme Court equated the Missouri Supreme Court's ruling to state action.

Indeed, the 14th Amendment prohibition that "No *state* ... shall ... deprive any person of ... property" was met when the Missouri court deprived the Shelleys of their property.

Although the contract itself was private, the plaintiff in the litigation had sought the assistance of the state court in enforcing the contractual provisions.

Chief Justice Vinson wrote: "[A]ction of State courts and of judicial officers in their official capacities is to be regarded as action of the State within the meaning of the Fourteenth Amendment." This meant the state could not be complicit in discriminatory private action violative of the 14th Amendment.

He concluded:

"We have no doubt that there has been State action in these cases in the full and complete sense of the phrase. The undisputed facts disclose that petitioners were willing purchasers of properties upon which they desired to establish homes. The owners of the properties were willing sellers; and contracts of sale were accordingly consummated. It is clear that but for the active intervention of the State courts, supported by the full panoply of State power, petitioners would have been free to occupy the properties in question without restraint." Accordingly, State judicial enforcement of restrictive covenants based on race denies the equal protection of laws in violation of the Fourteenth Amendment."

Racial restrictive covenants were common at one time in many American cities. Many old deeds still contain these restrictions, though Shelley v. Kraemer made them unenforceable.

Post Script. Private discrimination in housing is now prohibited by Title VIII of the Civil Rights Act of 1968, as well as by statutes in most States and by ordinances in many municipalities as well.

[Context: The seller, a White, sold to Shelley, a Black. Kraemer, a white neighbor, was too late to block the sale but now challenged the validity of Shelly's ownership. The Court found the covenant though private could only be enforced through state action prohibited by the 14th Amendment.]

Assignment

Brief the *Mendez* and *Shelley* cases using the FIRAC method of Facts, Issues, Rules, Arguments and Conclusion.

CHAPTER 7

Separate but Equal

Sweatt v. Painter (1950)

Heman Marion Sweatt (pronounced "sweet"), a black man, was refused admission to the School of Law of the University of Texas, whose president was Theophilus Painter, on the grounds that the Texas State Constitution prohibited integrated education.

The state district court in Travis County, Texas, continued the case for six months. This allowed the state time to build and staff a new law school for black-students-only in Houston. The white law school Sweatt applied to was in Austin.

The Texas trial court found against Sweatt, the Texas Appeals Court affirmed, and the Texas Supreme Court likewise denied Sweatt any relief. Sweatt, backed by the NAACP and represented by Robert L. Carter and Thurgood Marshall, petitioned the US Supreme Court.

The US Supreme Court reversed the Texas Supreme Court decision, finding the separate school failed to qualify, both in quantitative differences in facilities and experiential factors, including an isolation effect in keeping Black law students from inter-acting with White law students.

The court held that, when considering graduate education, experience must be considered as part of "substantive equality." The court's decision included differences identified between white and black facilities:

> The University of Texas Law School had 16 full-time and 3 part-time professors, while the Black law school had 5 full-time professors.
>
> The University of Texas Law School had 850 students and a law library of 65,000 volumes, while the Black law school had 23 students and a library of 16,500 volumes.
>
> The University of Texas Law School had moot court facilities, an Order of the Coif affiliation, and numerous graduates involved in public and private law practice, while the Black law school had only one practice court facility and only one graduate admitted to the Texas Bar.

These facts showed the Black law school was separate but not (qualitatively or experientially) equal to the White.

Sweatt was admitted to the White law school.

Post Script: On June 14, 2005, the Travis County Commissioners voted to rename the courthouse as The Heman Marion Sweatt Travis County Courthouse in Sweatt's honor.

[Context: This case is another step toward desegregation spear-headed by the NAACP. In prior cases the lack of any Black graduate or law school in a state assured a state's inability to meet the separate-but-equal requirements because the "separate" requirement alone was not met.

In this case the "separate" requirement was met but the "equal" requirement was not.

The NAACP had set a precedent in this case leaving it poised to attack nearly any segregated school system at any level in the United States because the buildings and books for Blacks all over the country were far worse than those for Whites. Black schools were separate but not equal.]

McLaurin v. Oklahoma State Regents (1950)

George W. McLaurin had a master's degree in education when he was denied admission to the University of Oklahoma to pursue a doctorate degree in the same discipline.

McLaurin successfully sued in the US District Court for the Western District of Oklahoma to gain admission to the institution basing his argument on the Fourteenth Amendment. But at the time Oklahoma law prohibited schools from instructing Blacks and Whites together.

The court found that the university's inaction in providing separate facilities, in order to meet Oklahoma state law, allowing McLaurin to attend the institution was a violation of his Constitutional rights. However, the court did not issue any injunctive relief as requested by the plaintiff instead relied "on the assumption that the law having been declared, the State will comply." But it did not.

The University admitted McLaurin but gave him a special table in the cafeteria, a designated desk in the library, and a desk just outside the classroom doorway.

McLaurin returned to the US District Court and petitioned to require the University of Oklahoma to allow him to interact with the other students fully. The court denied McLaurin's petition.

McLaurin then appealed to the US Supreme Court. On June 5, 1950, the Court ruled that a public institution of higher learning could not provide different treatment to a student solely because of his/her race because doing so deprived the student of his/her 14th Amendment rights of Equal Protection.

Accordingly, the high court reversed the decision of the US District Court, ordering the University of Oklahoma to remove the (isolating) restrictions McLaurin had been facing.

[Context: Hurdles to integration remained very high in the 1950s. The University of Oklahoma, an institution of higher learning, could have dignified McLauren's efforts to get a post-graduate degree but instead stuck him at tables and desks away from White students until the high court stepped in.]

Assignment

Make a list of the cases presented so far and describe what each one stands for in as few words as possible.

CHAPTER 8

Desegregation

Brown v. Board of Education (1954)

Historical Background: The Declaration of Independence stated "All men are created equal" but because of slavery this statement was not to be grounded in law in all states until after the Civil War.

In 1865 the Thirteenth Amendment was ratified to put an end to slavery. And soon after, the Fourteenth Amendment (1868) strengthened the legal rights of newly freed slaves by stating, among other things, that no state shall deprive any person due process of law or equal protection of the law. Lastly, the Fifteenth Amendment (1870) further strengthened the legal rights of newly freed slaves by prohibiting states from denying any male the right to vote due to race.

Despite these Amendments African Americans were treated differently than Whites. In fact, many state legislatures enacted laws that led to the legally mandated segregation of the races.

Laws of many states decreed that Blacks and Whites could not use the same public facilities, ride the same buses, attend the same schools, *etc.* And impediments to Black voting (violence, intimidation, reduced numbers of polling places, poll taxes and literacy tests) were instituted.

These laws came to be known as Jim Crow laws. They were unjust. The decision in *Plessy v. Ferguson (1896)* and the doctrine it adopted—separate but equal—emboldened Jim Crow lawmaking.

The NAACP founded on Abraham Lincoln's 100th birthday (February 12, 1909) developed a Legal Defense and Education Fund out of its grassroots contributions.

In the 1930s Charles Hamilton Houston of the NAACP launched a strategic attack against states without Black law schools and graduate schools to force them under the "separate but equal" doctrine to build law schools for Blacks or admit Blacks into already existing White schools. Thurgood Marshall, hired by Houston, argued the "separate but equal" doctrine.

Marshall had one success after another. The Court was finally coming around to what was plain as day in the 14th Amendment—equal protection of the law.

In 1954 the US Supreme Court heard five consolidated cases dealing with segregated public schools.

Evidence included a "doll test" with identical dolls (one Black and one White) to show segregated school systems had a tendency to make Black children feel inferior to White children. The test (from Mamie and Kenneth Clark—Black psychologists) turned on which doll a black child would assign positive traits to (Black children chose the White doll) and negative traits to (Black children chose the Black doll).

Every generation of Blacks in the US knew from early on where they stood in society. And the separate "education" they got did nothing to improve that standing.

On May 14, 1954, Chief Justice Earl Warren delivered the unanimous opinion of the Court, "We conclude that in the field of public education the doctrine of 'separate but equal' has no place. Separate educational facilities are inherently unequal..."

Expecting opposition to its ruling, especially in the southern states, the Supreme Court did not immediately try to implement the ruling.

The next year (1955) in a case called *Brown II* involving the same parties the issue of the failure of school districts to implement desegregation was heard. The Court empowered US District Courts to monitor state plans for desegregation to be carried out with all deliberate speed.

Although it would be many years before all segregated school systems were to be desegregated, *Brown* and *Brown II* (as the Court's plan for how to desegregate schools came to be called) were responsible for getting the process underway.

[Context: The South remained staunch in its refusal to integrate in 1954. In response the high court was finally legislating morality and opening the door to integration to better the education of people of color. Looming was the question whether the transition from segregation to integration would go smoothly.]

Cooper v. Aaron (1958)

After the *Brown v. Board of Education* decision was handed down from the United States Supreme Court in 1954, the Little Rock, Arkansas School District adopted a two-and-one-half year staged plan to desegregate public schools—first for high schools, then junior high schools and finally elementary schools.

But after *Brown* and *Brown II*, Arkansas (in 1956) defiantly amended its constitution opposing desegregation in the state. Arkansas also made a law relieving students from compulsory attendance at racially mixed schools.

At Central High School in Little Rock, Arkansas nine Black students (to become known as the Little Rock 9) were poised to start school on September 3, 1957.

The day before school the Governor of Arkansas, Orval Faubus, dispatched units of the Arkansas National Guard to the Central High School campus to block the black students from going to class. Violence appeared imminent.

The school board requested the Little Rock 9 stay away from school and the same day petitioned the District Court for an alternate course of action other than the original desegregation plan but the court refused.

The following day and for the next three weeks the Little Rock 9 were shut out by the Arkansas National Guard troops. The school board unsuccessfully petitioned the District Court for an order that would temporarily suspend the desegregation program.

In addition, the District Court requested the United States Attorney for the Eastern District of Arkansas to begin an immediate investigation to correct the interference with the court order to end segregation.

Following investigation, the District Court found that the Governor had disrupted the school board's plan by using National Guard troops and granted a preliminary injunction on September 20, 1957, preventing the Governor and National Guard from interfering with the orders of the court in carrying out the desegregation plan.

Beginning September 23, 1957, the Little Rock 9 entered the school, but later that day had to be removed by the Little Rock police due to demonstrations against them.

On September 25, 1957, the President of the United States (Dwight D. Eisenhower) sent federal troops to Central High School to facilitate admission of the Little Rock 9. In the end eight of them finished out the school year.

The school board and Superintendent of Schools filed a petition in District Court on February 20, 1958, requesting to postpone their program for desegregation based on public hostility fomented by the Governor and Legislature.

The District Court granted the postponement because of the turmoil and violence that was upsetting the students, teachers and parents. The Little Rock 9 filed an appeal to the US Court of Appeals and a petition for certiorari to the US Supreme Court. The Court of Appeals reversed the decision of the District Court. The petition for certiorari was granted, and the US Supreme Court reviewed the facts and affirmed the decision of the Court of Appeals.

The Supreme Court determined that the school board had demonstrated good faith in its attempts to carry out its plan of desegregation, and that the conditions at Central High School had caused the school to suffer. In making its decision, the Supreme Court applied the principle of the Fourteenth Amendment that no state shall deny any person within its jurisdiction the equal protection of the laws, thereby enforcing and reinstating the school board's plan for desegregation in compliance with the *Brown v. Board of Education* decision.

The Supreme Court denied the Arkansas School Board the right to delay desegregation for 30 months.

On September 12, 1958, the Warren Court handed down a *per curiam* (unanimous) decision. The Court held that the states are bound by the Court's decisions and must enforce them even if the states disagree with them.

The Court had the ultimate say.

Judicial supremacy was established in *Marbury v. Madison (1803)* a case of first impression where the Supreme Court determined it alone (and not Congress and not the President and not a State) had the last say as to which laws or Presidential conduct is constitutional or not. The ruling in *Marbury v. Madison* established what came to be known as the doctrine of judicial review.

Just because Congress or a state makes a law or the President makes an executive order does not make that law or order constitutional.

But the law or the order if challenged is subject to judicial review and in turn the court (not the legislature or executive) is the ultimate arbiter (decider) of the question of constitutionality.

The decision in this case upheld the rulings in *Brown v. Board of Education* and *Brown II* that the doctrine of separate but equal is unconstitutional and integration must proceed with all deliberate speed.

[Context: In *Brown* the Supreme Court unanimously ruled for integration of public schools in America. In response Arkansas directly defied the ruling amending its constitution to oppose desegregation and the governor ordered state national guard to block nine Black high schoolers from going to school with Whites. It took the President of the United States and federal troops to carry out the high court's ruling to integrate. And the ruling was final. Challenging it in court failed.]

Assignment

Provide brief biographies of the following individuals: Emmett Till, Rosa Parks, Medgar Evers, Martin Luther King, Jr., Malcolm X, John Lewis, Trayvon Martin and George Floyd; and, describe the origin and goal of "Black Lives Matter."

CHAPTER 9

Privacy

Olmstead v. United States (1928)

Roy Olmstead was a suspected bootlegger. Without judicial approval (*i.e.*, a search warrant), federal agents installed wiretaps in the basement of Olmstead's building (where he maintained an office) and in the streets near his home.

Olmstead was convicted of bootlegging with evidence obtained from the wiretaps.

This case was decided along with *Green v. United States*, in which Green and several other defendants were similarly convicted, based on illegally obtained wiretapped conversations, for conspiracy to violate the National Prohibition Act by importing, possessing, and selling illegal liquors. This case was also decided with *McInnis v. United States*.

The Court held that neither the Fourth nor Fifth Amendment rights of the wire-tapped (recorded) parties were violated. The majority concluded the use of wiretapped conversations as incriminating evidence did not violate their Fifth Amendment protection against self-incrimination because they were not forcibly or illegally made to conduct those conversations.

The Court, relying on prior case law, asserted that physical trespass by the federal agents into a home or office was required for a violation of the Fourth Amendment (illegal search and seizure). But here in the Olmstead case the physical trespass to the wires at points outside the home and office captured phone conversations within the home and office.

The Court noted the conversations were voluntarily made between the parties and their associates. Moreover, the Court went on, the parties' Fourth Amendment rights were not infringed because mere wiretapping does not constitute a search and seizure under the meaning of the Fourth Amendment.

The Court emphasized the Fourth Amendment covered an actual physical examination of one's person, papers, tangible material effects, or home—not their conversations. Finally, the Court added that while wiretapping may be unethical no court may exclude evidence solely for moral reasons.

When criticized for his opinion, Justice Taft mocked his foes. Writing to a friend he stated: "If they think we are going to be frightened in our effort to stand by the law and give the public a chance to punish criminals, they are mistaken, even though we are condemned for lack of high ideals."

Prior cases required physical intrusion without a warrant for a Fourth Amendment violation. But modern times and technology gave police the ability to trespass invisibly and listen in on all calls.

Listening in on private phone calls, a dissenting justice, Louis Brandeis, argued is more of an invasion of privacy than reading someone's mail because it goes to what people say and shows in more particular ways what they are thinking.

Brandeis delivered a historic dissent that articulated a constitutional right to privacy. Years before in 1890 Justice Brandeis had co-authored an article in the Harvard Law Review entitled "The Right to Privacy."

He summarized a person's right to be let alone:

> *"The makers of our Constitution undertook to secure conditions favorable to the pursuit of happiness* .... *They conferred, as against the Government, the right to be let alone—the most comprehensive of rights, and the right most valued by civilized men. To protect that right, every unjustifiable intrusion by the Government upon the privacy of the individual, whatever the means employed, must be deemed a violation of the Fourth Amendment."*

[Context: The majority was willing to ignore an individual's right to privacy rather than overturn a conviction. The majority used the artifice of no-physical-intrusion to allow an even greater kind of non-physical intrusion.

The minority ignored the character (physical or non-physical) of the intrusion, finding any governmental intrusion an unauthorized invasion of privacy. For the minority, absent exigent circumstances the government has to get a search warrant to avoid the Fourth Amendment prohibition against illegal search and seizure.]

Katz v. United States (1967)

In this case the Court redefined what constitutes "searches" and "seizures" with regard to the protections of the Fourth Amendment. It extended Fourth Amendment protection beyond the traditional confines of citizens' homes and property to anywhere a person has a reasonable expectation of privacy.

Katz overturned *Olmstead v. United States (1928)*. It also examined the notion of unreasonable intrusion by government or law enforcement. The *Katz* test of an actual expectation of privacy and one that society would find reasonable has been used in thousands of cases, particularly with the advancement of technology that pose new questions on expectations of privacy.

The case involved Charles Katz, a handicapper specializing in betting on college basketball. The FBI began investigating his gambling activities, and in 1965 secretly recorded him reporting his handicaps to bookmakers by means of a covert listening device the FBI had attached to a telephone booth near his apartment in Los Angeles.

FBI agents arrested Katz and charged him with transmitting wagers across US state lines over telephone in violation of US gambling law.

At trial, Katz's lawyer argued that the telephone booth he used should be considered a "constitutionally protected area" under the Fourth Amendment, and so the FBI's recordings of his conversations should be excluded as evidence because the FBI had not obtained a search warrant allowing them to place the listening device on the phone booth.

The judge rejected this argument, and Katz was convicted based on the recordings as evidence. Katz appealed to the US Supreme Court.

In December 1967, the Supreme Court issued a 7-1 decision in Katz's favor and overturned his conviction. Its decision redefined the law governing the Fourth Amendment's protections previously limited to searches and seizures of individuals' "persons, houses, papers, and effects" and previously interpreted to require an actual "trespass" or other physical intrusion by law enforcement officers.

The Court now expanded the Amendment's protections beyond those traditional areas, stating that "what [a person] seeks to preserve as private, even in an area accessible to the public, may be constitutionally protected."

[Context: An individual's expectation of privacy is a matter of personal freedom. It is the duty of the Court to make sure individual rights are protected against governmental interference. The government can seek a search warrant if it has probable cause to conduct a search of an individual but failing to do so violates due process and is an illegal search and invasion of privacy.]

Assignment

Review the Amendments to the Constitution from 1st to 27th, provide a brief description of each one and list the ones involving privacy.

CHAPTER 10

The Commerce Clause

Boynton v. Virginia (1960)

Bruce Boynton was a student at Howard University School of Law in Washington, D.C. travelling on a Trailways bus for a holiday trip to his home in Selma, Alabama.

The bus made a forty-minute stop in Richmond. Boynton went into a "Whites Only" restaurant in the terminal and ordered a cheeseburger and a hot tea. Authorities ordered him to go to the "Black" section. He said he had rights as an American to stay where he was and get served. They handcuffed him for misdemeanor trespass. He spent the night in jail and was fined $10.

The Court held that racial segregation in public transportation was illegal because such segregation violated the Interstate Commerce Act, forbidding discrimination in interstate passenger transportation. And the Court likewise noted bus transportation was sufficiently related to interstate commerce to allow Congress to regulate commerce and to forbid racial discrimination in the industry.

Post Script: This outlawing of racial segregation in public transportation led directly to a movement called the Freedom Riders. African Americans and Whites began to ride together on various forms of public transportation in the South to challenge local laws or customs that enforced segregation. Some riders were brutally murdered by Ku Klux Klansmen.

Attorney General Robert F. Kennedy confronted the Interstate Commerce Commission (ICC) with its failure to enforce prior bus desegregation rulings and forced the ICC to issue new regulations that effectively ended Jim Crow in public transportation.

[Context: Using the commerce clause (Const., Art. I, Sec. 8) to enforce equal rights was another way, besides the 14ᵗʰ Amendment, to fight racial inequality.]

Heart of Atlanta Motel, Inc. v. United States (1964)

This case challenged the Civil Rights Act of 1964, the first comprehensive act by Congress on civil rights and race relations since the Civil Rights Act of 1875.

For nearly one hundred years segregation thrived under the "separate but equal" doctrine relegating Blacks to inferior accommodations, services, and treatment.

Discrimination through private action continued to exist.

But Congress' power over interstate commerce became key to the Court's decision in the *Heart of Atlanta Motel* case. The motel was large (216 rooms) and its business relied on local and interstate travelers. Indeed, its guests and its business had a direct effect on interstate commerce.

Congress's power over interstate commerce comes directly from the commerce clause of the Constitution (Article I, Section 8) that authorizes Congress "to regulate Commerce with foreign Nations, and among the several States, and with Indian Tribes."

Title II of the Civil Rights Act of 1964 prohibits discrimination in public accommodations.

The owner of the motel sued the government claiming the act violated the commerce clause and he had a right to deny service to Blacks. His case was consolidated with a restaurant case likewise based on a refusal to serve Blacks.

The US Supreme Court held that Congress acted well within its authority under the Commerce Clause in passing the Civil Rights Act of 1964, thereby upholding the act's Title II in question.

While it might have been possible for Congress to pursue other methods for abolishing racial discrimination, the way Congress did, according to the Court, was perfectly valid.

[Context: Congress, in enacting the Civil Rights Act of 1964, gave people the tools for desegregation. Now they were locked in battle to make it happen.]

Assignment

Write biographies of James Chaney, Andrew Goodman, and Michael Schwerner.

CHAPTER 11

Privacy and Sex

Griswold v. Connecticut (1965)

This case is about access to contraception. It involves the right of privacy. Connecticut had a law, called the Comstock law, that prohibited any person from using "any drug, medicinal article or instrument for the purpose of preventing conception."

In the late 19th and early 20th century, physicians in the United States largely avoided the publication of any material related to birth control, even when they often recommended or at least gave advice regarding it to their married patients.

Then in 1914, Margaret Sanger, a proponent of birth control, openly challenged the public consensus against contraception. She influenced the Connecticut Birth Control League (CBCL) and helped to develop the eventual concept of the Planned Parenthood clinics.

The first Planned Parenthood clinic in Connecticut opened in 1935 in Hartford. It provided services to women who had no access to a gynecologist, including information about artificial contraception and other methods to plan the growth of their families. Several clinics were opened in Connecticut over the following years, including the Waterbury clinic that led to this legal dispute.

In 1939 this clinic was compelled to enforce the 1879 anti-contraception law. This caught the attention of the CBCL leaders, who were promoting the importance of birth control.

During the 1940s several cases arose involving the Waterbury clinic, leading to legal challenges to the constitutionality of the Comstock law but the cases failed on technicalities.

Finally, in this case (*Griswold v. Connecticut (1965)*) the Supreme Court held that the statute was unconstitutional, and that "the clear effect of [the Connecticut law ...] is to deny disadvantaged citizens ... access to medical assistance and up-to-date information in respect to proper methods of birth control."

By a vote of 7–2, the US Supreme Court invalidated the law on the grounds that it violated the "right to marital privacy", establishing the basis for the right to privacy with respect to intimate practices. It recognized the basic need for protection from governmental intrusion.

The Court could not point to a constitutional provision specifically mentioning personal privacy. It was not in the Constitution. Looking for something to hang the Court's hat on Justice William O. Douglas waxed prosaic musing the right of privacy existed in the "penumbras" and "emanations" of the Constitution, *i.e.*, in the immediate perimeter of the blend of shadow, light and aura surrounding the Constitution—not literally in the Constitution but figuratively at its immediate fringe.

Another justice relied on the Ninth Amendment—a catch-all amendment that gave constitutional protection to unidentified and unenumerated fundamental rights not specifically expressed in the Constitution.

Other justices floated the notion that privacy was protected by the due process clause of the Fourteenth Amendment.

In any event common sense dictates personal freedom has to include the fundamental right of privacy especially in intimate relationships—without governmental interference.

[Context: Personal privacy is so obviously and clearly an element of personal freedom that it might just have been that in 1787 the Framers naturally overlooked it or took it as a given with no need to mention it in the Constitution. Privacy was so basic and fundamental a right it went unmentioned again in the Bill of Rights (1791). A right to privacy was indirectly referenced in the 3rd Amendment regarding quartering of soldiers and more directly in the 4th Amendment regarding illegal search and seizure but lawmakers then, including descendants of Puritans, did not appear to have had an appetite to expressly constitutionalize such an obvious right covering private or intimate acts.]

Loving v. Virginia (1967)

This case involved Mildred Loving, a woman of color, and her white husband Richard Loving, who in 1958 were sentenced to a year in prison for marrying each other.

Their marriage violated Virginia's Racial Integrity Act of 1924, that criminalized marriage between people classified as "white" and people classified as "colored". The Lovings appealed their conviction to the Supreme Court of Virginia and it was upheld. They then appealed to the US Supreme Court.

On June 12, 1967 the Court issued a unanimous decision in the Lovings' favor and overturned their convictions. The Court struck down Virginia's anti-miscegenation law ending all race-based legal restrictions on marriage in the United States.

Virginia had argued that its law was not a violation of the Equal Protection Clause because the punishment was the same regardless of the offender's race, and thus it "equally burdened" both whites and non-whites. [Equal punishment is a far cry from an equal right.]

The Court found that the law nonetheless violated the Equal Protection Clause because it was based solely on "distinctions drawn according to race" and outlawed conduct—namely, getting married—that was otherwise generally accepted and which citizens were free to do.

Anti-miscegenation laws in the United States had been in place in certain states since colonial days. In the Reconstruction Era in 1865, the Black Codes across the seven states of the lower South made intermarriage illegal.

In 1967, before the *Loving* decision 16 Southern states had anti-miscegenation laws.

[Context: The Civil Rights Act of 1964 and Voting Rights Act of 1965 ushered in a new era of civil rights similar to the one that stalled in Reconstruction against the rise of the KKK immediately after the Civil War and took another nosedive with separate-but-equal in 1896.

The 1960s were a new chance for America to live up to its ideals. This time the Supreme Court supported rather than stymied those ideals. It was time to tear up anti-miscegenation laws and dignify inter-racial marriage.

It was time to tell Southern states they had no right to tell anyone who to marry. The old laws were a clear example of governmental interference into personal freedom.]

Assignment

Summarize the key provisions of the Civil Rights Act of 1964.

CHAPTER 12

Discrimination

Jones v. Alfred H. Mayer Co. (1968)

[Quoting from the case]

The Civil Rights Act of 1968 allows the federal government to ban private parties from engaging in discriminatory housing policies.

Petitioners, alleging that respondents had refused to sell them a home for the sole reason that petitioner Joseph Lee Jones is a Negro, filed a complaint in the District Court, seeking injunctive and other relief.

Petitioners relied in part upon 42 USC § 1982, which provides that all citizens "shall have the same right, in every State and Territory, as is enjoyed by white citizens thereof to inherit, purchase, lease, sell, hold, and convey real and personal property."

The District Court dismissed the complaint, and the Court of Appeals affirmed, concluding that § 1982 applies only to state action, and does not reach private refusals to sell.

Held:

1. Congress' enactment of the Civil Rights Act of 1968, containing in Title VIII detailed housing provisions applicable to a broad range of discriminatory practices and enforceable by a complete arsenal of federal authority, had no effect upon this litigation or upon § 1982, a general statute limited to racial discrimination in the sale and rental of property and enforceable only by private parties acting on their own initiative. Pp. 392 U. S. 413–417.

2. Section 1982 applies to all racial discrimination in the sale or rental of property. Pp. 392 U. S. 417–437.

   (a) Section 1982 has previously been construed to do more than grant Negro citizens the general legal capacity to buy and rent property free of prohibitions that wholly disable them because of their race. Hurd v. Hodge, 334 U. S. 24. Pp. 392 U. S. 417–419.

   (b) The question whether purely private discrimination, unaided by any governmental action, violates § 1982 remains one of first impression in this *Court. Hurd v. Hodge, supra*; *Corrigan v. Buckley*, 271 U. S. 323; the *Civil Rights Cases*, 109 U. S. 3, and *Virginia v. Rives*, 100 U. S. 313, distinguished. Pp. 392 U. S. 419–420.

   (c) On its face, the language of § 1982 appears to prohibit all discrimination against Negroes in the sale or rental of property. Pp. 392 U. S. 420–422.

   (d) The legislative history of § 1982, which was part of § 1 of the Civil Rights Act of 1866, likewise shows that both Houses of Congress believed that they were enacting a comprehensive statute forbidding every form of racial discrimination affecting the basic civil rights enumerated therein—including the right to purchase or lease property—and thereby securing all such rights against interference from any source whatever, whether governmental or private.

(e) The scope of the 1866 Act was not altered when it was reenacted in 1870, two years after ratification of the Fourteenth Amendment.

(f) That § 1982 lay partially dormant for many years does not diminish its force today.

3. Congress has power under the Thirteenth Amendment to do what 42 USC. § 1982 purports to do.

(a) Because the Thirteenth Amendment "is not a mere prohibition of State laws establishing or upholding slavery, but an absolute declaration that slavery or involuntary servitude shall not exist in any part of the United States," *Civil Rights Cases*, 109 U. S. 3, 109 U. S. 20, it has never been doubted "that the power vested in Congress to enforce the article by appropriate legislation," ibid., includes the power to enact laws "operating upon the acts of individuals, whether sanctioned by State legislation or not." Id. at 109 U. S. 23. *See Clyatt v. United States*, 197 U. S. 207. P. 392 U. S. 438.

(b) The Thirteenth Amendment authorized Congress to do more than merely dissolve the legal bond by which the Negro slave was held to his master; it gave Congress the power rationally to determine what are the badges and the incidents of slavery and the authority to translate that determination into effective legislation.

(c) Whatever else they may have encompassed, the badges and incidents of slavery that the Thirteenth Amendment empowered Congress to eliminate included restraints upon "those fundamental rights which are the essence of civil freedom, namely, the same right ... to inherit, purchase, lease, sell and convey property, as is enjoyed by white citizens." *Civil Rights Cases*, 109 U. S. 3, 109 U. S. 22. Insofar as *Hodges v. United States*, 203 U. S. 1, suggests a contrary holding, it is overruled.

MR. JUSTICE DOUGLAS, concurring.

The Act of April 9, 1866, 14 Stat. 27, 42 USC. § 1982, provides:

> "All citizens of the United States shall have the same right,
> in every State and Territory, as is enjoyed by white citizens
> thereof to inherit, purchase, lease, sell, hold, and convey real
> and personal property."

This Act was passed to enforce the Thirteenth Amendment, which, in § 1, abolished "slavery" and "involuntary servitude, except as a punishment for crime whereof the party shall have been duly convicted" and, in § 2, gave Congress power "to enforce this article by appropriate legislation."

Enabling a Negro to buy and sell real and personal property is a removal of one of many badges of slavery.

"Slaves were not considered men .... They could own nothing; they could make no contracts; they could hold no property, nor traffic in property; they could not hire out; they could not legally marry nor constitute families; they could not control their children; they could not appeal from their master; they could be punished at will."

W. Dubois, *Black Reconstruction in America* 10 (1964). [Footnote 2/1] ...

Some badges of slavery remain today. While the institution has been outlawed, it has remained in the minds and hearts of many white men. Cases which have come to this Court depict a spectacle of slavery unwilling to die. We have seen contrivances by States designed to thwart Negro voting, *e.g., Lane v. Wilson*, 307 U. S. 268. Negroes have been excluded over and again from juries solely on account of their race, *e.g., Strauder v. West Virginia*, 100 U. S. 303, or have been forced to sit in segregated seats in courtrooms, *Johnson v. Virginia*, 373 U. S. 61. They have been made to attend segregated and inferior schools, *e.g., Brown v. Board of Education*, 347 U. S. 483, or been denied entrance to colleges or graduate schools because of their color, *e.g., Pennsylvania v. Board of Trusts*, 353 U. S. 230; *Sweatt v. Painter*, 339 U. S. 629. Negroes have been prosecuted for marrying whites, *e.g., Loving v. Virginia*, 388 U. S. 1. They have been forced to live in segregated residential districts, *Buchanan v. Warley*, 245 U. S. 60, and residents of white neighborhoods have denied them entrance, *e.g., Shelley v. Kraemer*, 334 U. S. 1. Negroes have been forced to use segregated facilities in going about their daily lives, having been excluded from railway coaches, *Plessy v. Ferguson*, 163 U. S. 537; public parks, *New Orleans Park Improvement Assn. v. Detiege*, 358 U. S. 54; restaurants, *Lombard v. Louisiana*, 373 U. S. 267; public beaches, *Mayor of Baltimore v. Dawson*, 350 US 877; municipal golf courses, *Holmes v. City of Atlanta*, 350 US 879; amusement parks, *Griffin v. Maryland*, 378 U. S. 130; buses, *Gayle v. Browder*, 352 US 903; public libraries, *Brown v. Louisiana*, 383 U. S. 131. A state court judge in Alabama convicted a Negro woman of contempt of court because she refused to answer him when he addressed her as "Mary," although she had made the simple request to be called "Miss Hamilton." *Hamilton v. Alabama*, 376 U. S. 650.

That brief sampling of discriminatory practices, many of which continue today, stands almost as an annotation to what Frederick Douglass (1817–1895) wrote nearly a century earlier:

"Of all the races and varieties of men which have suffered from this feeling, the colored people of this country have endured most. They can resort to no disguises which will enable them to escape its deadly aim. They carry in front the evidence which marks them for persecution. They stand at the extreme point of difference from the Caucasian race, and their African origin can be instantly recognized, though they may be several removes from the typical African race. They may remonstrate like Shylock—"

"Hath not a Jew eyes? hath not a Jew hands, organs, dimensions, senses, affections, passions? fed with the same food, hurt with the same weapons, subject to the same diseases, healed by the same means, warmed and cooled by the same summer and winter, as a Christian is?"

"—but such eloquence is unavailing. They are Negroes—and that is enough, in the eye of this unreasoning prejudice, to justify indignity and violence. In nearly every department of American life, they are confronted by this insidious influence. It fills the air. It meets them at the workshop and factory, when they apply for work. It meets them at the church, at the hotel, at the ballot box, and, worst of all, it meets them in the jury box. Without crime or offense against law or gospel, the colored man is the Jean Valjean of American society. He has escaped from the galleys, and hence all presumptions are against him. The workshop denies him work, and the inn denies him shelter; the ballot box a fair vote, and the jury box a fair trial. He has ceased to be the slave of an individual, but has, in some sense, become the slave of society. He may not now be bought and sold like a beast in the market, but he is the trammeled victim of a prejudice, well calculated to repress his manly ambition, paralyze his energies, and make him a dejected and spiritless man, if not a sullen enemy to society, fit to prey upon life and property and to make trouble generally. [Footnote 2/2]"

Today the black is protected by a host of civil rights laws. But the forces of discrimination are still strong.

A member of his race, duly elected by the people to a state legislature, is barred from that assembly because of his views on the Vietnam war. *Bond v. Floyd*, 385 U. S. 116.

Real estate agents use artifice to avoid selling "white property" to the blacks. [Footnote 2/3] The blacks who travel the country, though entitled by law to the facilities for sleeping and dining that are offered all tourists, *Heart of Atlanta Motel v. United States*, 379 U. S. 241, may well learn that the "vacancy" sign does not mean what it says, especially if the motel has a swimming pool. On entering a half-empty restaurant, they may find "reserved" signs on all unoccupied tables. The black is often barred from a labor union because of his race. [Footnote 2/4] He learns that the order directing admission of his children into white schools has not been obeyed "with all deliberate speed," *Brown v. Board of Education*, 349 U. S. 294, 349 U. S. 301, but has been delayed by numerous stratagems and devices. [Footnote 2/5] State laws, at times, have even encouraged discrimination in housing. *Reitman v. Mulkey*, 387 U. S. 369.

This recital is enough to show how prejudices, once part and parcel of slavery, still persist. The men who sat in Congress in 1866 were trying to remove some of the badges or "customs" [Footnote 2/6] of slavery when they enacted § 1982. And, as my Brother STEWART shows, the Congress that passed the so-called Open Housing Act in 1968 did not undercut any of the grounds on which § 1982 rests.

[Footnote 2/1]

The cases are collected in five volumes in H. Catterall, *Judicial Cases Concerning American Slavery and the Negro* (1926–1937). And see 1 T. Cobb, *An Inquiry into the Law of Negro Slavery*, c. XIV (1858); G. Ostrander, *The Rights of Man in America* 1606–1861, p. 252 (1960); G. Stroud, Sketch of the Laws Relating to Slavery 45–50 (1827); J. Wheeler, *Law of Slavery* 190–191 (1837).

[Footnote 2/2]

Excerpt from Frederick Douglass, *The Color Line, The North American Review*, June 1881, 4 *The Life and Writings of Frederick Douglass* 343–344 (1955).

[Footnote 2/3]

See Kamper v. Department of State of New York, 22 N.Y.2d 690, 238 N.E.2d 914.

[Footnote 2/4]

See, e.g., O'Hanlon, *The Case Against the Unions, Fortune,* Jan.1968, at 170.

[Footnote 2/5]

The contrivances which some States have concocted to thwart the command of our decision in *Brown v. Board of Education* are by now legendary. *See, e.g., Monroe v. Board of Commissioners,* 391 U. S. 450 (Tennessee "free-transfer" plan); *Green v. County School Board,* 391 U. S. 430 (Virginia school board "freedom of choice" plan); *Raney v. Board of Education,* 391 U. S. 443 (Arkansas "freedom of choice" plan); *Bradley v. School Board,* 382 U. S. 103 (allocation of faculty allegedly on a racial basis); *Griffin v. School Board,* 377 U. S. 218 (closing of public schools in Prince Edward County, Virginia, with tuition grants and tax concessions used to assist white children attending private segregated schools); *Goss v. Board of Education,* 373 U. S. 683 (Tennessee rezoning of school districts, with a transfer plan permitting transfer by students on the basis of race); *United States v. Jefferson County Board of Education,* 372 F.2d 836, aff'd en banc, 380 F.2d 385 (C.A. 5th Cir.1967) ("freedom of choice" plans in States within the jurisdiction of the United States Court of Appeals for the Fifth Circuit); *Northcross v. Board of Education,* 302 F.2d 818 (C.A. 6th Cir.1962) (Tennessee pupil assignment law); *Orleans Parish School Board v. Bush,* 242 F.2d 156 (C.A. 5th Cir.1957) (Louisiana pupil assignment law); *Hall v. St. Helena Parish School Board,* 197 F. Supp. 649 (D.C.E.D.La.1961), aff'd, 368 U. S. 515 (Louisiana law permitting closing of public schools, with extensive state aid going to private segregated schools); *Holmes v. Danner,* 191 F. Supp. 394 (D.C.M.D. Ga.1961) (Georgia statute cutting off state funds if Negroes admitted to state university); *Aaron v. McKinley,* 173 F. Supp. 944 (D.C.E.D. Ark.1959), aff'd sub nom. *Faubus v. Aaron,* 361 U. S. 197 (Arkansas statute cutting off state funds to integrated school districts); *James v. Almond,* 170 F. Supp. 331 (D.C.E.D.Va.1959) (closing of all integrated public schools).

See also Rogers v. Paul, 382 U. S. 198; *Calhoun v. Latimer*, 377 U. S. 263; *Cooper v. Aaron*, 358 U. S. 1.

[Footnote 2/6]

My Brother HARLAN's listing of some of the "customs" prevailing in the North at the time § 1982 was first enacted shows the extent of organized white discrimination against newly freed blacks. As he states, "[r]esidential segregation was the prevailing pattern almost everywhere in the North." Post at 392 U. S. 474–475. Certainly, then, it was "customary." To suggest, however, that there might be room for argument in this case (post at 392 U. S. 475, n. 65) that the discrimination against petitioners was not in some measure a part and product of this longstanding and widespread customary pattern is to pervert the problem by allowing the legal mind to draw lines and make distinctions that have no place in the jurisprudence of a nation striving to rejoin the human race."

[Context: What stands out is the Court's recognition of all the bad rulings and decisions on civil rights over many decades, all the ways the courts were complicit in limiting the rights of minorities and keeping them down, undereducated, impoverished and politically powerless. This case shows how America historically had been unable to shake its *Original Sin*—Slavery—or the badges of slavery.

The prior cases identified in this one effectively kept the black man down for over 100 years after the Civil War. Here finally a black man got the US Supreme Court to protect Black home ownership.]

Griggs v. Duke Power Company (1971)

In the 1950s Duke Power's Dan River Steam Station in North Carolina had a policy restricting black employees to its "Labor" department, where the highest-paying position there paid less than the lowest-paying position in its four other departments.

In 1955 the company added the requirement of a high school diploma for employment in any department other than Labor, and offered to pay two-thirds of the high-school training tuition for employees without a diploma.

On July 2, 1965 the day the Civil Rights Act of 1964 took effect Duke Power added two employment tests, which would allow employees without high-school diplomas to transfer to higher-paying departments. The Bennett Mechanical Comprehension Test was a test of mechanical aptitude, and the Wonderlic Cognitive Ability Test was an IQ test measuring general intelligence.

Blacks were almost ten times less likely than whites to meet these new employment and transfer requirements. According to the 1960 Census, while 34% of white males in North Carolina had high-school diplomas, only 18% of blacks did. The disparities of aptitude tests were far greater; with the cutoffs set at the median for high-school graduates, 58% of whites passed, compared to 6% of blacks.

The Supreme Court ruled that under Title VII of the Civil Rights Act of 1964, if such tests disparately impact ethnic minority groups businesses must demonstrate that such tests are "reasonably related" to the job for which the test is required.

[Quoting from the case:] "Because Title VII was passed pursuant to Congress's power under the Commerce Clause of the Constitution, the disparate impact test later articulated by the Supreme Court in *Washington v. Davis*, 426 US 229 (1976) is inapplicable. (The *Washington v. Davis* test for disparate impact is used in constitutional equal protection clause cases, while Title VII's prohibition on disparate impact is a statutory mandate.)

"As such, Title VII of the Civil Rights Act prohibits employment tests (when used as a decisive factor in employment decisions) that are not a "reasonable measure of job performance," regardless of the absence of actual intent to discriminate. Since the aptitude tests involved, and the high school diploma requirement, were broad-based and not directly related to the jobs performed, Duke Power's employee transfer procedure was found by the Court to be in violation of the Act.

"The Court of Appeals' opinion, and the partial dissent, agreed that, on the record in the present case, "whites register far better on the Company's alternative requirements" than Negroes. This consequence would appear to be directly traceable to race. Basic intelligence must have the means of articulation to manifest itself fairly in a testing process.

"Because they are Negroes, petitioners have long received inferior education in segregated schools, and this Court expressly recognized these differences in *Gaston County v. United States,* 395 US 285 (1969). There, because of the inferior education received by Negroes in North Carolina, this Court barred the institution of a literacy test for voter registration on the ground that the test would abridge the right to vote indirectly on account of race.

"Congress did not intend by Title VII, however, to guarantee a job to every person regardless of qualifications. In short, the Act does not command that any person be hired simply because he was formerly the subject of discrimination, or because he is a member of a minority group. Discriminatory preference for any group, minority or majority, is precisely and only what Congress has proscribed. What is required by Congress is the removal of artificial, arbitrary, and unnecessary barriers to employment when the barriers operate invidiously to discriminate on the basis of racial or other impermissible classification.

"On the record, neither the high school completion requirement nor the general intelligence test is shown to bear a demonstrable relationship to successful performance of the jobs for which it was used. Both were adopted, as the Court of Appeals noted, without meaningful study of their relationship to job performance ability. Rather, a vice-president of the Company testified, the requirements were instituted on the Company's judgment that they generally would improve the overall quality of the workforce.

"The evidence, however, shows that employees who have not completed high school or taken the tests have continued to perform satisfactorily, and make progress in departments for which the high school and test criteria are now used.

"The promotion record of present employees who would not be able to meet the new criteria thus suggests the possibility that the requirements may not be needed even for the limited purpose of preserving the avowed policy of advancement within the Company. In the context of this case, it is unnecessary to reach the question whether testing requirements that take into account capability for the next succeeding position or related future promotion might be utilized upon a showing that such long-range requirements fulfill a genuine business need. In the present case, the Company has made no such showing.

"The Court of Appeals held that the Company had adopted the diploma and test requirements without any "intention to discriminate against Negro employees." 420 F.2d at 1232. We do not suggest that either the District Court or the Court of Appeals erred in examining the employer's intent; but good intent or absence of discriminatory intent does not redeem employment procedures or testing mechanisms that operate as "built-in headwinds" for minority groups and are unrelated to measuring job capability."

[Context: Title VII of the Civil Rights Act of 1964 protects workers from invidious discrimination based on race. Employers who put up barriers to employment had to show the barrier did not have a disparate (uneven or unequal) impact on persons of any one race to the benefit or detriment of another.

In this case the barriers were two tests (IQ and aptitude) that had no rational relationship to the jobs offered but provided the employer with a pretext to promote Whites over Blacks and keep Blacks as a labor force likely never to reach managerial positions—in other words—to racially discriminate against them in the workplace.

Whether or not the employer here truly intended to discriminate does not matter when the result of its conduct is racial discrimination. This conduct violated the Civil Rights Act.]

Ledbetter v. Goodyear (2007)

This was a case of statutory rather than constitutional interpretation, explaining the meaning of a law, not its constitutionality. The plaintiff in this case, Lilly Ledbetter, characterized her situation as one where "disparate pay is received during the statutory limitations period, but is the result of intentionally discriminatory pay decisions that occurred outside the limitations period."

The law in question states:

"It shall be an unlawful employment practice for an employer ... —to discriminate against any individual with respect to his compensation, terms, conditions, or privileges of employment, because of such individual's race, color, religion, sex, or national origin ...."

"A charge under this section shall be filed within one hundred and eighty days after the alleged unlawful employment practice occurred."

"[I]t shall not be an unlawful employment practice for an employer to apply different standards of compensation ... provided that such differences are not the result of an intention to discriminate because of race, color, religion, sex, or national origin."

In rejecting Ledbetter's appeal, the Supreme Court said that "she could have, and should have, sued" when the pay decisions were made, instead of waiting beyond the 180-day statutory charging period. The Court did leave open the possibility that a plaintiff could sue beyond the 180-day period if she did not, and could not, have discovered the discrimination earlier. The effect of the Court's holding was reversed by the passage of the Lilly Ledbetter Fair Pay Act in 2009.

In 1979 Lilly Ledbetter, the plaintiff, began work at the Goodyear Tire and Rubber Company in its Gadsden, Alabama location, a union plant. She started with the same pay as male employees, but by retirement, she was earning $3,727 per month compared to 15 men who earned from $4,286 per month (lowest paid man) to $5,236 per month (highest paid man).

During her years at the factory as a salaried worker, raises were given and denied based partly on evaluations and recommendations regarding worker performance. From 1979–1981 Ledbetter received a series of negative evaluations, which she later claimed were discriminatory. Although her subsequent evaluations were good, in part as a result of those early negative evaluations, her pay never reached the level of similar male employees.

All merit increases had to be substantiated by a formal evaluation. In March 1998, Ledbetter inquired into the possible sexual discrimination of the Goodyear Tire Company. In July she filed formal charges with the Equal Employment Opportunity Commission. In November 1998, after early retirement, Ledbetter sued claiming pay discrimination under Title VII of the Civil Rights Act of 1964 and the Equal Pay Act of 1963. The Supreme Court did not rule on whether this was discrimination, just the statute of limitations to sue.

Post script: In 2007, several Democratic members of Congress introduced the Lilly Ledbetter Fair Pay Act, which revised the law to state that if a present act of discrimination pertains, prior acts outside of the 180-day statute of limitations for pay discrimination can be incorporated into the claim.

In January 2009, Congress passed and President Obama signed into law the Lilly Ledbetter Fair Pay Act.

[Context: Plaintiff, a woman, was doing the same jobs as men but paid less. Getting less pay for the same jobs was sex (gender) discrimination. The employer had strict rules that employees could only discuss wage and salary details with the employer and no one else. The disparity in pay here—except for its fluke discovery—would never have been known. The company here was saved by the 180-day statute of limitations for filing a claim.]

Assignment

Brief, using the FIRAC method, the case of *Gaston County v. United States*, 395 U.S. 285 (1969).

CHAPTER 13

Abortion

Roe v. Wade (1973)

The United States Supreme Court ruled (7–2) that unduly restrictive state regulation of abortion is unconstitutional. In a majority opinion the court held that a set of Texas statutes criminalizing abortion in most instances violated a woman's constitutional right of privacy.

The Court based its decision on a constitutionally implied right of privacy first recognized in *Griswold v. Connecticut (1965)*.

Keeping her identity secret given the extremely private nature of the lawsuit, Norma McCorvey, proceeded under the fictitious legal name "Roe" in a federal action against Henry Wade, the district attorney of Dallas county, Texas, where Roe resided.

The Supreme Court disagreed with Roe's assertion of a woman's absolute right to terminate a pregnancy and attempted to balance a woman's right of privacy with a state's interest in regulating abortion.

States' police powers cover their citizens' health, safety, morals and welfare.

In his opinion, Justice Harry Blackmun noted that only a "compelling state interest" justifies regulations limiting "fundamental rights" such as privacy and that legislators must therefore draw statutes narrowly "to express only the legitimate state interests at stake."

The Court then attempted to balance the state's distinct interests—both compelling—in the health of pregnant women and in the potential life of fetuses.

The Court left it to the woman to make a decision on abortion during the first three months (trimester) of the pregnancy. But the Court acknowledged the state's compelling interest beginning after the first trimester.

With regard to the state's interest in protecting a fetus it began when the fetus was capable "of meaningful life outside the mother's womb," or put another way, viable.

Repeated challenges since 1973 narrowed the scope of *Roe* v. *Wade* but did not overturn it.

Historically, abortion was not only legal but also not widely considered immoral in the 1700s and the early to mid-1800s in the United States. Only in the late 1800s did doctors and the Roman Catholic Church take a stand against it.

Although by the early 1900s all US states had outlawed abortion, these bans were rarely enforced until the late 1930s.

Abortion restrictions were lifted in California and New York long before *Roe v. Wade*. Texas law before *Roe v. Wade* prohibited abortion unless the mother's life was at stake.

[Context: The right of privacy includes the right to control one's body and make health choices. A pregnant woman controls her body and that of a fetus. It is a moral and legal question if a woman decides to terminate a pregnancy and abort a fetus.

Under law a fetus becomes a person even when it is in the womb when it has developed sufficiently to live outside the womb (*i.e.*, viable). The state has an interest in the health of the mother and in the health of the child.

Control belongs solely to the mother until the child is viable. The state allows the mother full control to abort for the first trimester but, after that, abortion is only legal to preserve the health of the mother.]

Planned Parenthood v. Casey (1992)

In this case the Court upheld the constitutional right to have an abortion that was established in *Roe v. Wade* (1973) but altered the standard for analyzing restrictions on that right, crafting the undue burden standard for abortion restrictions.

The case arose from a challenge to five provisions of the Pennsylvania Abortion Control Act of 1982. Among the provisions were requirements for a waiting period, spousal notice, and (for minors) parental consent prior to undergoing an abortion procedure.

The Supreme Court upheld the "essential holding" of *Roe*, which was that the due process clause of the Fourteenth Amendment protects a woman's right to choose to have an abortion prior to viability of the fetus.

The Court overturned the *Roe* trimester framework in favor of a viability analysis, thereby allowing states to implement abortion restrictions that apply during the first trimester of pregnancy.

The Court also replaced the strict scrutiny standard of review required by *Roe* with the undue burden standard, where abortion restrictions would be unconstitutional when they were enacted for "the purpose or effect of placing a substantial obstacle in the path of a woman seeking an abortion of a nonviable fetus."

Applying this new standard of review, the Court upheld four provisions of the Pennsylvania law, but invalidated the requirement of spousal notification.

Post Script: Later in *Gonzales v. Carhart* (2007), the court upheld the federal Partial-Birth Abortion Ban Act (2003), which prohibited a rarely used abortion procedure known as intact dilation and evacuation.

In *Whole Woman's Health* v. *Hellerstedt* (2016), the court invoked its decision in *Casey* to strike down two provisions of a Texas law that had required abortion clinics to meet the standards of ambulatory surgical centers and abortion doctors to have admitting privileges at a nearby hospital. These requirements disqualified certain abortion clinics and made it more difficult for women to get an abortion.

Again, in 2020 the Supreme Court struck down a Louisiana law similar to the Texas law in *June Medical Services v. Russo*.

[Context: While the state has a compelling interest in a child in a womb capable of being born alive it cannot create undue burdens to a woman getting an abortion.]

Assignment

Brief *June Medical Services v. Russo (2020)*.

CHAPTER 14

(Gender) Sex Equality

Phillips v. Martin Marietta Corp. (1971)

This is an early sex discrimination case under Title VII of the Civil Rights Act of 1964.

Title VII prohibits discrimination by covered employers on the basis of race, color, religion, sex or national origin (*see* 42 USC. § 2000e-2).

Title VII applies to and covers an employer "who has fifteen (15) or more employees for each working day in each of twenty or more calendar weeks in the current or preceding calendar year" as written in the Definitions section (*see* 42 USC. § 2000e-(b)).

Title VII also prohibits discrimination against an individual because of his or her association with another individual of a particular race, color, religion, sex, or national origin, such as by an interracial marriage.

Title VII has also been supplemented with legislation prohibiting pregnancy, age, and disability discrimination (*see* Pregnancy

Discrimination Act of 1978, Age Discrimination in Employment Act, and Americans with Disabilities Act of 1990).

The Martin Marietta Corporation had a policy not to hire mothers with pre-school aged children because they were assumed to be unreliable employees.

Ida Phillips, a mother, applied for a job at the company and did not get it. Phillips sued under Title VII claiming the policy was discriminatory.

An employer may not, in the absence of business necessity, refuse to hire women with pre-school-age children while hiring men with such children.

The US Supreme Court unanimously held that Marietta's policy discriminated on the basis of sex, overturned the lower court, and sent the case back to the lower court for trial while suggesting the employer may be able to justify the discrimination using the Bona Fide Occupational Qualifications (BFOQ) Exception.

[Context: Equality in the workplace is a matter of fundamental fairness. American custom and practice recognized for a long time that it was a white man's world with all power, wealth and decision-making in his control. Title VII levels the playing field for men and women and stands for no discrimination on the basis of sex.]

Frontiero v. Richardson (1973)

Appellant, a married woman Air Force officer sought increased benefits for her husband as a "dependent" under 37 USC §§ 401, 403, and 10 USC §§ 1072 1076.

These statutes allow (female) spouses of male members of the uniformed services increased quarters allowances and medical and dental benefits but deny (male) spouses of female members the same benefits unless the male spouse depends on the female spouse for more than half his support.

When her application was denied because her husband relied on her for less than half his support she and her husband sued in federal district court on the ground the federal statutes deprived servicewomen of due process. That court ruled against her and her husband.

The US Supreme Court considered whether due process applied to discrimination actions brought on the basis of sex (gender) as it had on the basis of race.

The US Supreme Court had developed a formula where laws discriminating against a suspect class (persons of color) could only be upheld for a compelling state interest (usually to promote its citizens' health, safety, morals or welfare) and the law in question had to have been narrowly drawn using the least restrictive means to effect that interest.

The question before the Court concerned laws drawn by the government affecting the right of a female member of the uniformed services to claim her spouse as a "dependent" for the purposes of obtaining increased quarters' allowances and medical and dental benefits on an equal footing with male members.

The statutes allow a serviceman to claim his wife as a "dependent" without regard to whether she is dependent on him for any part of her support. A servicewoman, on the other hand, is not allowed to claim her husband as a "dependent" unless he is dependent on her for over one-half of his support. Inequality based on sex (gender) seems readily apparent here.

Does the difference in treatment amount to unconstitutional discrimination against a woman in violation of the Due Process Clause of the Fifth Amendment?

A man gets the benefits with no hoops to jump through, but a woman only gets them after she jumps through the hoops.

Although these benefits would automatically go to the wife of a male member of the uniformed services, appellant's application was denied because she failed to show her husband was dependent on her for more than one-half of his support.

The alleged discrimination points out a woman's burdens under the statutes to (1) show her husband's dependency when a man would not have to, and (2) the man gets the benefits even if he does not provide more than half his wife's support when a woman in his shoes would not. The imbalance or inequality is apparent.

Appellants argue that classifications based on sex, like classifications based on race, alienage, and national origin, are inherently suspect, subjecting them to close judicial scrutiny.

The majority of the Court agreed, acknowledging the inequality and issued a permanent injunction against the continued enforcement of these statutes and ordered Lieutenant Frontiero be provided with the same housing and medical benefits that a similarly situated male member would receive.

[Context: Because sex (gender) is a suspect classification laws discriminating based on sex must be strictly scrutinized by the Court.

Strict scrutiny is the highest and most stringent standard of judicial review, and results in a judge striking down a law unless the government can demonstrate in court that a law or regulation: (1) is necessary to a "compelling state interest"; (2) that the law is "narrowly tailored" to achieving this compelling purpose; and (3) that the law uses the "least restrictive means" to achieve the purpose.

Intermediate scrutiny is the second level of deciding issues using judicial review. In order to overcome the intermediate scrutiny test, it must be shown that the law or policy being challenged furthers an important government interest by means that are substantially related to that interest.

It is part of the hierarchy of standards that courts use to determine which is weightier: a constitutional right or principle, or the government's interest against observance of the principle.

The least strict standard of review is called *Rational Basis Review*. It is the standard used to test statutes and government action at all levels of government within the United States. It requires the law or policy be rationally related to a legitimate government interest. This approach is most often employed in reviewing limits on commercial speech, and content-neutral regulations of speech.

Here the Court concluded there was no compelling interest to apply a law that differentiated between a man and a woman.]

Assignment

Identify and describe two other US Supreme Court cases decided on the basis of sex.

CHAPTER 15

Burning the Flag, Sexual Orientation, and Voting

Texas v. Johnson (1989)

Protestors gathered outside the Republican National Convention in Dallas in 1984. Gregory Lee Johnson was there to show his disapproval of President Reagan's policies by burning an American flag outside of the convention center.

This led to his conviction of a Texas statute preventing desecration of a venerated object when aimed at inciting anger in others.

On appeal, Johnson argued his actions were "symbolic speech" protected by the First Amendment.

The Justices on the Supreme Court decried the burning as an affront to those who had died for their country and the dissent argued the flag's unique status as a symbol of national unity outweighed "symbolic speech" concerns, and thus, the government could lawfully prohibit flag burning.

But the 5-4 majority concluded freedom of speech protects actions that society may find very offensive, but society's outrage alone is not justification for suppressing free speech where it does not actually incite violence.

[Context: If a person cannot peacefully protest even though it offends a vast majority of citizens then there is no such thing as "free speech." In a free society the right to criticize government without inciting riots must be unfettered, or the society is not free but oppressive.]

Romer v. Evans (1996)

Colorado voters adopted Amendment 2 to their State Constitution precluding any judicial, legislative, or executive action designed to protect persons from discrimination based on their "homosexual, lesbian, or bisexual orientation, conduct, practices or relationships."

Following a legal challenge by homosexual and other aggrieved parties, the state trial court entered a permanent injunction enjoining Amendment 2's enforcement. The Colorado Supreme Court affirmed on appeal.

The US Supreme Court held that Amendment 2 of the Colorado State Constitution violated the equal protection clause. Amendment 2 singled out homosexual and bisexual persons, imposing on them a broad disability by denying them the right to seek and receive specific legal protection from discrimination.

In his opinion for the Court, Justice Anthony Kennedy noted that oftentimes a law will be sustained under the equal protection clause, even if it seems to disadvantage a specific group, so long as it can be shown to "advance a legitimate government interest."

Amendment 2, by depriving persons of equal protection under the law due to their sexual orientation failed to advance such a legitimate interest. Justice Kennedy concluded: "If the constitutional conception of 'equal protection of the laws' means anything, it must at the very least mean that a bare desire to harm a politically unpopular group cannot constitute a legitimate governmental interest."

[Context: Making a law aimed at a particular group is suspect. Equal protection blankets all persons—*all*—without exclusion. Absent a compelling state interest, it is unconstitutional to discriminate against any particular group.]

Shelby County of Alabama v. Holder (2013)

This case involves the Voting Rights Act of 1965 enacted to end voter discrimination based on race, color or membership in a language minority group.

Under a prescribed formula certain voting districts (with histories of voter suppression) were to have changes in voter laws pre-cleared by the US Attorney General or a 3-Judge Panel of the DC District Court.

Targeted districts were found in whole or part in all Southern states, New York, California, South Dakota, Michigan, Arizona and Alaska.

Shelby County challenged the more than 40-year old formula identifying which voting districts needed pre-clearance to change their voting rules—and the Court agreed that it was no longer an effective formula and unconstitutional—and invited Congress to step up to change it.

But the Republican run Congress has failed to do it. The net effect of the decision has allowed additional impediments to voting including requiring voter IDs and poll closings predominantly in minority communities. Unless and until the Democrats gain power in both House and Senate nothing will change.

Quoting the Court, "Although the constraints this section places on specific states made sense in the 1960s and 1970s, they do not any longer and now represent an unconstitutional violation of the power to regulate elections that the Constitution reserves for the states."

The Court also held that the formula for determining whether changes to a state's voting procedure should be federally reviewed is now outdated and does not reflect the changes that have occurred in the last 50 years in narrowing the voting turnout gap in the states in question.

Justice Ruth Bader Ginsburg wrote a dissent concluding evidence Congress gathered to determine whether to renew the Voting Rights Act sufficiently proved that there was still a current need to justify the burdens placed on the states in question.

[Context: States continue to manipulate voting along partisan lines. Republicans make it as difficult as possible; Democrats, as easy.]

Obergefell v. Hodges (2015)

[Largely in the language of the Court]

Michigan, Kentucky, Ohio, and Tennessee defined marriage as a union between one man and one woman. Plaintiffs challenged the laws as violating the Fourteenth Amendment. The district courts ruled in their favor. The Sixth Circuit consolidated the cases and reversed. The Supreme Court reversed.

The Fourteenth Amendment requires a state to license a marriage between two people of the same sex and to recognize a marriage between two people of the same sex when their marriage was lawfully licensed and performed out-of-state.

The Court noted other changes in the institution of marriage: the decline of arranged marriages, invalidation of bans on interracial marriage and use of contraception, and abandonment of the law of coverture.

The fundamental liberties protected by the Fourteenth Amendment extend to certain personal choices central to individual dignity and autonomy, including intimate choices defining personal identity and beliefs. Marriage is a centerpiece of social order and fundamental under the Constitution; it draws meaning from related rights of childrearing, procreation, and education. The marriage laws at issue harm and humiliate the children of same-sex couples; burden the liberty of same-sex couples; and abridge central precepts of equality.

There may be an initial inclination to await further legislation, litigation, and debate, but referenda, legislative debates, and grassroots campaigns; studies and other writings; and extensive litigation have led to an enhanced understanding of the issue. While the Constitution contemplates that democracy is the appropriate process for change, individuals who are harmed need not await legislative action before asserting a fundamental right. The First Amendment ensures that religions, those who adhere to religious doctrines, and others have protection as they seek to teach the principles that are central to their lives and faiths.

In Ohio, John Arthur was suffering from the latter stages of amyotrophic lateral sclerosis (ALS), a terminal illness. Recognizing the need to make critical end-of-life decisions, Arthur sought to have the Ohio Registrar identify his partner, James Obergefell, as his surviving spouse on his death certificate so that Obergefell could receive the benefits due to a spouse. Arthur and Obergefell had married in Maryland two years earlier. The Registrar planned to certify Obergefell as Arthur's spouse on the death certificate, believing that discrimination against same-sex couples was unconstitutional. The state of Ohio prohibited same-sex marriage, however, and its Attorney General's Office mobilized to defend that ban.

Also in Ohio, four same-sex couples brought a claim seeking the right to list both parents on the birth certificates of their children. In this case, known as Henry v. Wymyslo, three of the couples lived in Ohio, and all of the children were born there. Henry v. Wymyslo was heard before the same judge who reviewed the Obergefell case, District Judge Timothy S. Black.

In Tennessee, four same-sex couples sued to force the state to recognize their marriages, which had been performed in California and New York. (One of the New York couples later left the case.) They argued that Tennessee's refusal to recognize same-sex marriages violated its own rule that a marriage validated where it is celebrated is valid everywhere.

In Michigan, April DeBoer and Jayne Rowse brought a claim on behalf of themselves and three children whom they sought to jointly adopt. All of the children, one boy and two girls, had special needs. The two nurses challenged a state law prohibiting adoption by same-sex couples and limiting second-parent adoption to married couples, while defining marriage as between opposite-sex individuals only.

In Kentucky, Gregory Bourke and Michael DeLeon brought a claim on behalf of themselves and DeLeon's two adopted children. Three other couples, one with four children, joined their claim. While Bourke and DeLeon were legally married in Ontario, Canada, the other couples were married in Iowa, California, and Connecticut.

The couples prevailed in the federal district courts of all four states. In *Obergefell*, District Judge Black issued a temporary restraining order, which the state did not appeal, and planned oral arguments on whether a permanent injunction should be granted. Unfortunately, Arthur died before arguments were held, and the state moved within a week to dismiss the case as moot. Black denied the motion and ruled two months later that Ohio must recognize same-sex marriages performed in other states on death certificates. He also issued an order in *Henry v. Wymyslo* that required states to recognize same-sex marriages performed in other states, although he stayed the enforcement of his ruling with respect to matters other than the birth certificates sought in this specific case.

All four of these cases were appealed to the Sixth Circuit, which reversed the trial court decisions in each of them and reinstated the state bans on same-sex marriage. (Some observers, including the dissenting justice in the Sixth Circuit's 2-1 decision, speculated that the court took this view deliberately to force the Supreme Court to resolve the ensuing circuit split and provide a definitive answer on the issue of marriage equality.) The Supreme Court then consolidated the cases for review. Since the federal government previously had announced its support for marriage equality, US Solicitor General Donald Verrilli, Jr. joined the plaintiffs' lawyers for oral argument before the Court.

The majority opinion found marriage central to personal identity, dignity, and autonomy. Thus, it is a fundamental right that has strong protections under the Fourteenth Amendment, both independently and through its connection to related fundamental rights regarding child-rearing, procreation, and education. State bans on same-sex marriage clearly infringe on all of these rights by restricting the liberty of same-sex couples, harming the development of their children, and undermining principles of equality that lie at the core of American society.

Over time, this institution has evolved significantly from its traditional origins.

Archaic practices such as arranged marriages and the law of coverture have been abandoned. This Court has struck down state bans on the use of contraception (*see Griswold v. Connecticut*, 381 US 479 (1965)) and on interracial marriage (*see Loving v. Virginia*, 388 US 1 (1967)). There is no longer a reason to hesitate before recognizing the right of same-sex couples to marriage equality, for the merits of the issue have become abundantly clear through legislative debates, academic research, and a long history of litigation. Legislative action through the democratic process is the usual mechanism for change, but courts may intervene on behalf of people whose fundamental rights have been infringed. Granting marriage equality to same-sex couples accords them the equal dignity under the law to which they are constitutionally entitled.

The dissent argued the decision should not be made by the Court. It should be left to legislatures, as demonstrated by the writings of the Framers and earlier decisions of this Court. The majority has engaged in inappropriate judicial activism by taking this issue out of their hands. States should be free to define marriage as they see fit.

Post Script: The United States became the 23rd country to recognize marriage equality, joining Argentina, Belgium, Brazil, Canada, Denmark, the United Kingdom (except for Northern Ireland), Finland, France, French Guiana, Greenland, Iceland, Ireland, Luxembourg, Mexico, the Netherlands, New Zealand, Norway, Portugal, South Africa, Spain, Sweden, and Uruguay.

[Context: Every person is entitled to life, liberty and property. Fundamentally, from the liberty standpoint, that means everyone should be able to love and marry whomever they please.

Is it right for the state to limit, based on gender, the right to marry? Five out of nine justices said NO. Here again the Court was playing catch-up to the majority sentiment of the people in the country favoring same-sex marriage.]

Bostock v. Clayton County, Georgia (2020), Altitude Express v. Zarda (2020), R.G. & G.R. Harris Funeral Homes v. EEOC (2020) [3 Consolidated Supreme Court Cases]

Facts: Gerald Bostock claimed he was fired from his job as a social worker in Clayton County, Ga., after he became more open about being gay, including joining a gay softball league.

Donald Zarda said he was fired as a skydiving instructor after joking with a female client to whom he was strapped for a tandem dive that he was gay.

Aimee Stephens worked for years at a Michigan funeral home before being fired after informing the owners and colleagues of her gender transition.

Issue: Can an employer fire someone simply for being homosexual or transgender?

Rule: Title VII of the Civil Rights Act of 1964

Argument: Title VII prohibits discrimination "because of sex." The word "sex" has meant "gender" in most cases decided under Title VII. The fact pattern in those cases typically show treatment of a woman different from a man.

In general, discrimination can be in terms of jobs, pay, and benefits, *e.g.*, a woman is denied a job as a firefighter, or if she gets the job—gets paid 70 cents on a dollar compared to a man, and in terms of perks her out-of-town advanced training session results in a per diem less than her male counterpart.

Here people were fired because of their sexual orientation and transgender status.

The parties were joined in their arguments by notable entities and attacked by others. More than 70 friend-of-the-court briefs were filed, dividing states, religious orders and members of Congress. More than 200 of the nation's largest employers supported the workers here not their employers.

In contrast the Trump administration sided with the employers and against the workers, a position that put it at odds with the Equal Employment Opportunity Commission (EEOC), which decided in 2015 that gay and transgender people were federally protected.

Treating a man who is attracted to men differently from a woman who is attracted to men is discrimination, the EEOC reasoned.

The commission also looked at a 1989 Supreme Court decision that said federal law protected against discrimination based on stereotypes; the court found for a woman who had not been promoted because her employers found her too aggressive and her manner of dress not feminine enough.

That is analogous to discriminating against a transgender person for not conforming to norms expected of a gender, the commission said. Discrimination because of sexual orientation is the same thing, the EEOC said, because it relies on stereotypes about to whom men and women should be attracted.

Most appellate courts had come to agree with the EEOC, even when they had not done so in the past.

The full U.S. Court of Appeals for the 2nd Circuit ruled for Zarda and said its contrary past decisions on the issue were wrong. Chief Judge Robert A. Katzmann wrote that "sexual orientation discrimination is motivated, at least in part, by sex and is thus a subset of sex discrimination."

The U.S. Court of Appeals for the 6th Circuit came to a similar conclusion in Stephens's case. The panel found it "analytically impossible to fire an employee based on that employee's status as a transgender person without being motivated, at least in part, by the employee's sex."

But in Bostock's case, the U.S. Court of Appeals for the 11th Circuit went the other way, ruling for Clayton County, a suburb south of Atlanta, that Title VII did not protect on the basis of sexual orientation.

Gay rights leaders say "married on Sunday, fired on Monday" is a possibility in more than half of the United States, where there is no specific protection for gay or transgender workers. The states that prohibit discrimination are not uniform—some protect only gender identity or transgender status, and some differentiate between public and private employment.

Since the case was argued, Virginia became the most recent state to extend protection on its own.

Astonishingly, the dissent argued sexual orientation is something brand new to lawmakers not even considered in 1964 at the time of the Civil Rights Act (so the Act cannot possibly extend to sexual orientation) and going forward it should be up to legislators, not the Court, to decide the issue.

Conclusion: Under Title VII sexual orientation is protected from discrimination from employers.

[Context: Getting fired from a job based on sexual orientation is unfair. It is clearly a deprivation of property (one's livelihood) and a denial of equal protection when others with so-called normative sexual orientation are not fired.

Lesbians, Gays, Bisexuals, Transgenders and those Questioning their own sexuality (LGBTQ) have been the objects of ridicule by society and religion.

Some persons have used the term "Queer" instead of "Questioning." Queer had long been a slur for a "homosexual." "Queer" now serves as an umbrella term that encompasses many people as it intersects with sexual orientation and gender identity. It includes anyone who does not associate with heteronormativity, rather they have non-binary or gender expansive identities.

Title VII prohibits discrimination "on the basis of sex." This case sees "sex" not as gender only but as sexual orientation as well. Discrimination cannot be leveled against any human being based on their gender or sexual orientation.]

Assignment

(1) Describe the Equality Act of 2019 passed by the Democratic-led House of Representatives but stalled in the Republican-led Senate; and (2) write biographies of Matthew Shepard and Elijah McClain.

CHAPTER 16

Native Americans and DACA

United States v. Sioux Nation of Indians (1980)

After the Civil War the US Army turned to fighting the Powder River War of 1866–1867. Chief Red Cloud of the Sioux tribes fought to protect Sioux land protected by treaty from white settlement.

Military action ended with the Fort Laramie Treaty of April 29, 1868 pledging the Great Sioux Reservation of the Black Hills to be set apart for "the absolute and undisturbed use and occupation of the Indians."

By the terms of the treaty, no more land would be given up except by a new treaty executed and signed by at least three fourths of all the adult male Indians occupying the land.

The treaty brought peace for several years.

But white settlement was soon stirred by the Army and condoned by the President (Grant).

In 1874 on rumors of gold Army General George Armstrong Custer led an exploratory expedition into the Black Hills. Custer and his wife, Libby, promoted through news dispatches and articles the mineral and timber resources of the Black Hills, and its suitability for grazing and cultivation.

This ignited a popular demand for opening the Black Hills for settlement. And Whites went there.

At first they were turned away by the military. But soon Grant, the Secretary of the Interior, and the Secretary of War, decided that the military should make no further resistance to the occupation of the Black Hills by miners. These orders were to be enforced quietly and the President's decision was to remain confidential.

Additional settlers and gold miners went to the Black Hills. The Government believed, despite the treaty, it should leave settlers alone and get the land back from the Sioux. It appointed a commission to negotiate a purchase.

Negotiations failed.

The Government took to military force. It created a pretext claiming the Sioux were hostile when they did not return from an off-reservation hunting expedition in the dead of winter when travel was impossible.

A military expedition was mounted to remove the Sioux from the Black Hills. It included an attack on an Indian village on the Little Bighorn River by Custer.

Sioux, led by Chiefs Sitting Bull and Crazy Horse, wiped out Custer and the 7th Cavalry Regiment (Custer's Last Stand).

Libby spent the rest of her days on circuit tours and in writings publicly lamenting these facts and fomenting hatred of the Indian.

The victory over Custer only led to more soldiers expanding the Army's ranks and more battles. In the end surviving Indians surrendered to the Army, to be interned on reservations, disarmed and dependent on rations from the Government stripped of dignity and their way of life.

In 1876 Congress threatened to cut off money for subsistence to the Sioux Indians unless they gave up the Black Hills to the US.

To avoid starvation a few of the Sioux but not enough to make it effective under the Laramie Treaty signed a new treaty to transfer the land.

Congress approved the Indian Appropriations Bill of 1876 denying the Sioux all further appropriation and treaty-guaranteed annuities ($) until they gave up the Black Hills.

The Sioux never accepted the legitimacy of the forced deprivation of their Black Hills reservation. In 1920 lobbyists for the Sioux persuaded Congress to authorize a lawsuit against the United States in US Claims Court. The Sioux filed a petition in 1923, but the Claims Court dismissed the case in 1942, holding that the Court could not second guess whether their compensation was adequate.

The Sioux (and many other tribes) continued lobbying Congress for a forum for their claims, and in 1946 Congress created an independent federal agency, the Indian Claims Commission to hear and determine all tribal grievances including the Sioux claim.

The Sioux lost their first hearing before the Indian Claims Commission but on appeal to the US Claims Court, the Court directed the Commission to take new evidence. Legal wrangling went on from 1958 to 1972 when the Commission ruled in favor of the Sioux, awarding damages for the deprivation of the land, but not interest.

Findings concluded the US acquired the Black Hills through a course of outrageous, unfair and dishonorable dealing shamelessly underpinning the Sioux's entitlement to damages.

The finding of "no interest" had already been adjudicated so the Sioux were barred from relitigating the issue under the doctrine of *res judicata* (once an issue in a case is finally determined (tried) it cannot be retried).

In 1978 Sioux lobbyists persuaded Congress to pass yet another law conferring authority on the Claims Court to hear the Sioux case, this time without regard to *res judicata*. That meant the Sioux could re-litigate the claim for 100 years' worth of interest.

Finally, under its new authorizing statute, the Claims Court held the Sioux had suffered a taking cognizable under the Fifth Amendment (deprivation of property without due process), and were entitled to the value of the land as of the 1877 taking which was $17.1 million, the value of gold prospectors illegally took out of the land computed at $450,000, and 100 years' worth of interest at 5% per year which would be an additional $88 million.

This holding the Government appealed, and the US Supreme Court granted the petition for writ of certiorari. Justice Blackmun delivered the Court's opinion in which six other justices joined. Justice White concurred in part, and Justice Rehnquist dissented.

The issue was whether the Sioux had already been awarded just compensation for their land, and the Court affirmed the Claims Court's decision that they never had been. The court found Congress had dual conflicting roles: one, the benevolent trustee for Indians; but two, empowered to take Indian land.

Any taking by Congress had to be in good faith but the taking of Sioux land had not been.

So the Court ordered under the 5ᵗʰ Amendment the payment of just compensation for the taking of the land. It affirmed the ruling allowing interest.

Associate Justice William Rehnquist alone dissented, arguing Congress overstepped its authority going beyond the bounds of separation of powers by interfering with the earlier court decision on no-interest that should have been *res judicata*.

He found the Sioux were adequately compensated a hundred years before and new times or *mores* should not upset prior findings. Put another way, the remedy for a harm done in the distant past should fade away over time.

Post Script: The Sioux have declined to accept the money because, they concluded, acceptance would legally terminate Sioux demands for return of the Black Hills. The money remains in a Bureau of Indian Affairs account accruing compound interest.

In lieu of accepting the payment outlined in the court settlement, Sioux leaders created the Black Hills Steering Committee, a political group consisting of members from each Sioux tribe that coalesced around the shared goal of pressuring Congress to enact legislation that would reestablish Sioux sovereignty over the Black Hills territory. But internal differences on the committee have prevented a precise action despite some potential Congressional support.

[Context: The Plains Indian stood in the way of US expansion. Buying land was one way to get it. But if Indians did not want to sell what was the proper solution? Was it war? It was war. Was there justification? The US employed a doctrine called Manifest Destiny—the supposed inevitability of the continued territorial expansion of the boundaries of the United States westward to the Pacific.

Before the Civil War the idea of Manifest Destiny was used to validate continental acquisitions in the Oregon Country, Texas, New Mexico and California. The purchase of Alaska after the Civil War briefly revived the concept of Manifest Destiny. And it rose its head again in the 1890s, when the country went to war with Spain, annexed Hawaii, and laid plans for an isthmian canal across Central America.

Whites simply believed they had a God-given right to expand the footprint of the country and anyone in their way would have to go along or "git" along. Refusal by the Indians to sell their land was met by US Army offensives leading to Indian deaths and later to dependency on a government that could not be trusted.]

Department of Homeland Security v. Regents of the University of California (2020)

This case involves an Executive Order of President Barack Obama. His successor in office (Donald Trump) rescinded the order.

The question for the Court was limited to whether Trump's rescission was valid—not whether the original order was valid.

Executive Orders have the effect of law. They allow a President to make law in areas where the executive is empowered to do so—such as matters of immigration. By contrast, a President cannot declare war or control government spending—only Congress can. And both executive orders and acts of Congress are subject to judicial review. A President can rescind an executive order.

Obama's 2012 executive order gave temporary protection from deportation to persons brought here illegally as children, mostly from Mexico and Central America. The order was called DACA (Deferred Action for Childhood Arrivals).

The DACA program gave childhood arrivals temporary legal status if they graduated from high school or were honorably discharged from the military, and if they passed a background check. Some 800,000 persons qualified. They have been called "Dreamers" because they are seeking the American Dream.

Chief Justice Roberts, in a 5–4 decision wrote the majority opinion—a narrow but powerful rejection of the way the Trump administration went about trying to abolish DACA.

Roberts found the Trump administration could not give a reasoned explanation for its action. In 2017, then-Attorney General Jeff Sessions simply declared DACA illegal and unconstitutional. Sessions said of Obama's order, "Such an open-ended circumvention of immigration laws was an unconstitutional exercise of authority by the executive branch." Sessions argued that the program should be rescinded calling it unlawful from the start.

The attorney general offered no detailed justifications for canceling DACA. Nor did the acting Secretary of Homeland Security at the time, Elaine Duke, who put out a memo announcing the rescission of DACA that relied entirely on Sessions' opinion that the program was unlawful.

Duke's memo did not address the fact that thousands of young people (living in fear of deportation) had come to rely on the program, emerging from the shadows to enroll in degree programs, embark on careers, start businesses, buy homes and even marry and have 200,000 children of their own who are U.S. citizens, not to mention that DACA recipients pay $60 billion in taxes each year.

Roberts found these factors significant and deserving of comment by the Trump administration if it were to abolish DACA.

The outright failure to address these concerns made the briefly worded statement to abolish DACA "arbitrary and capricious." That means it was based on individual discretion rather than a fair application of the law and it resulted from a sudden and unaccountable change of mood.

The administration invented arguments against court challenges after the rescission. These after-the-fact justifications included a memo issued by then-Secretary of Homeland Security Kirstjen Nielsen that Roberts found too little, too late.

An agency must defend its action based on the reasons it gave at the time it acted—not when the case is already in court.

Roberts pointed out how wrongheaded the administration was. Instead of properly exercising its authority to rescind and taking responsibility for doing so the administration based its action on a preposterous claim that the Obama administration created what the Trump administration called an "illegal and unconstitutional" program.

The chief justice did not address that issue. Instead, he relied on commentary from immigration law professor Lucas Guttentag that the justices in the majority seemed to be saying, "Why should the court be the bad guy" when the administration "won't take responsibility" for rescinding DACA by explaining clearly what the policy justifications for the revocation are?

[Context: With Joe Biden beating Donald Trump efforts to protect Dreamers will continue. Further action will depend on modifications to the executive order or new congressional legislation.]

Assignment

Make an argument for giving Dreamers immediate US Citizenship.

Conclusion

There is no conclusion. Fairness and justice are democratic ideals. They are achieved by treating everyone the same under the law. America has opted for these ideals.

But historically America saw fit to allow slavery, take Indian land, start a war with Mexico for western land, and allow Whites to dominate Native Americans, Blacks, Hispanics and Asians.

"EQUAL JUSTICE UNDER LAW" was carved out of stone above the entrance to the US Supreme Court, finished in 1935.

It took even longer for that court to apply that phrase to actual cases.

Yet the whole time, those denied justice, kept fighting for it.

And the fight goes on.

www.ingramcontent.com/pod-product-compliance
Lightning Source LLC
Chambersburg PA
CBHW061259220326
41599CB00028B/5707